P9-BVF-956

were it not for grace

stories from **women after God's own heart**

were it not for grace

featuring Condoleezza Rice,
First Lady Laura Bush,
Beth Moore & others

as told by Leslie Montgomery

Nashville, Tennessee

Printed in the United States of America

Ten-digit ISBN: 0805431780
Thirteen-digit ISBN: 9780805431780

Published by Broadman & Holman Publishers,
Nashville, Tennessee

Dewey Decimal Classification: 248.843
Subject Heading: WOMEN \ CHRISTIAN LIFE

1 2 3 4 5 6 7 8 9 10 09 08 07 06 05

Dedication

I DEDICATE THIS BOOK to my dad, Arthur Baird Montgomery, who, against the advice of many, adopted me as his daughter years ago. It is because of your hope, faith, and love that I went from being a broken, rebellious child into a woman after God's own heart. God used you to prepare me to receive Christ as my Savior. For that I am eternally grateful. It was your example, unconditional love, and respect for me, despite my history, that led me to believe that God could love me too.

You're the best dad that any girl, anywhere, any time ever had.

Additionally, this book is dedicated to my Savior, Jesus Christ, to whom I am eternally indebted. I thank you, Lord, for giving me the privilege to suffer, because without those experiences I would not be the woman I am, nor would I have the intimacy with you and the passion for you that I do.

Thank Yous

I COULD NOT JUSTIFIABLY write this book without thanking some of the instrumental women after God's own heart who have led the way for me in my personal life:

Betty Tyndall—You will always be my spiritual mother. Not one day goes by that I don't thank God for you. Thank you for letting me cry (a lot) and for teaching me to find my voice.

Janice Cathey—Who lost her physical battle October 7, 2004, to cancer, but won the spiritual race. She *never* wavered in her walk with Christ, and her example will be forever embedded in my heart.

Shirley Robbins—Not many people have a psychologist of their own who is also their sister! Oh the stories you could tell (please don't)! I love you.

Cindy Reed—My sister who shares my passion for Christ and for restoration in the lives of broken women.

Mom—Thank you for always brushing my hair out of my eyes with your gentle hands so that I could see clearly. It worked.

To the women who participated in this project—Every one of your stories challenged, encouraged, and comforted me in the Lord. Thank you for being so honest and vulnerable for the sake of other women who are hurting.

Table of Contents

I consider that our present sufferings are not worth comparing with the glory that will be revealed in us.

Romans 8:18

Introduction

WHO IS A WOMAN after God's own heart? What does she look like, and where does she live? Is she single or married, with or without children, rich or poor, black or white, Methodist or Baptist? Is she tall or short, thin or heavy, blonde or brunette? As I pondered these questions after conducting the research and the interviews for this book, I found this woman to be in abundance on Earth. She is the woman who struggles with her identity, has a husband who struggles with pornography, has endured sexual abuse, has lost a child to death, has been called names and physically harmed, has dealt with anger and depression, and often lives with regrets from her past. I found her to be both black and white, dark and light haired, young and old, a variety of denominations, and scattered across the world.

While all of the women featured are different in various ways, they are all the same in one universal way: They love the Lord with all their hearts. Their souls thirst to know him, and therefore they don't settle for just knowing a lot about him. They have intimacy with him. They have an intimacy that didn't come without cost.

As I read and reread these stories, I considered some of the women who are mentioned in the Bible: Mary Magdalene, Joanna, and Susanna, who were among the "certain women who had been healed of evil spirits and infirmities" (Luke 8:1–3 NKJV); Martha, who was more practical than spiritual; Leah, who was not loved by her husband (Gen. 29:31); Tamar, who was raped by her stepbrother (Gen. 13); Elizabeth, who was childless the first ninety years of her life (Luke 1:7–25); Esther, who lived with prejudice (Esther 2–7); Hannah, who was barren (1 Sam.); Hagar, who was used (Gen. 16); Rachel, who was deceived (Gen. 29); Rahab, the prostitute (Josh. 2:1, 3) and the "woman . . . taken in adultery" (John 8:1–11 KJV). Some of these women were blameless, others suffered as a result of their own actions, but all of the women were worthy enough to be mentioned in God's Word for one reason: their story would impact women around the world for thousands of years to come.

The women in this book have a story to tell, one that you may be able to relate to, learn from, and use as an example in your own life or in the life of a friend or relative. Whether you struggle as a direct result of someone else's actions, as is the case with Beth Moore and Kay Coles James, or your struggle is a result of your own sin—which, by the way, is often the result of unresolved issues from someone else's actions—you can overcome it in Christ. No other answer will work.

You, too, can be a woman after God's own heart. It's not a secret that remains hidden or cannot be told. As a matter of fact, it's something that needs to be shouted from the rooftops. To be a woman after God's own heart, you have to possess what I call the four *S*s.

First, a woman after God's own heart realizes that she has a perpetual problem called sin and is therefore a *sinner.* She recognizes that she has chosen to do what she knows is wrong, and thus her sin has caused separation from God. She understands Romans 3:23

and 6:23: "For all have sinned and fall short of the glory of God. . . . The wages of sin is death, but the gift of God is eternal life in Christ Jesus our Lord."

The second thing a woman after God's own heart does is to recognize that there is only one way for her sin to be atoned, and that is through a *Savior.* She realizes that Jesus Christ came to Earth to die on the cross to pay the penalty for her actions. She knows that Jesus died for her because he loves her and he doesn't want her separated from him and that God, her Father, supernaturally raised Jesus from the dead. John 3:16 is her eternal lifeline: "For God so loved the world that he gave his one and only Son, that whoever believes in him shall not perish but have eternal life."

Next, a woman after God's own heart accepts his purpose for her life, which is *salvation.* She has to accept God's offer to be in an intimate relationship with him. In doing so, she is continually learning to trust him, rely on him, and seek him to satisfy the deepest hungers of her heart. She believes his Word in Jeremiah 29:11: "'For I know the plans I have for you,' declares the LORD, 'plans to prosper you and not to harm you, plans to give you hope and a future.'"

Finally, because of Jesus' sacrifice, she is willing to *surrender* herself and her life to Jesus Christ, relying on him alone as her personal Lord and Savior, giving him total control of every area of her life, recognizing Ephesians 2:8–9 to be a balm for her broken soul: "For it is by grace you have been saved, through faith—and this not from yourselves, it is the gift of God—not by works, so that no one can boast."

Are you a woman after God's own heart? If so, you too have a story to tell. I'd love for you to share it with me. Every woman who is a believer has a story of the tragedy of sin and the triumph of

Calvary. This triumph you've encountered is a process Scripture refers to as *sanctification.* Just like the women featured in this book, through Christ you will find freedom from the difficulties of life.

If you are not a woman after God's own heart, you can be. If the Lord is leading you now to enter into intimacy with him, you can cry out to him in prayer, and he will answer you. It's a simple process and does not need to be formal or legalistic. Just tell him what's on your heart. You might say something like: *God, I admit I am a sinner and have chosen my desires over you. I believe that Jesus died on the cross for me. Please forgive me for all my sins. Jesus, come into my life to be my Lord and Savior. Take control of my life and make me the person you want me to be. Thank you, Jesus, for what you will do in me, to me, and through me. In Jesus' name I pray, Amen.*

If you prayed that prayer, John 5:24 says you have crossed over from death to life. You have now become a woman after God's own heart. This is a decision that every one of the women featured in this book has made, and this has become their secret to overcoming difficult circumstances or tragedies in their lives. These women are often looked up to as spiritual giants; they have walked difficult paths of self-sacrifice to overcome some horrendous circumstances. You can too. Whatever you've experienced in your past or are experiencing now, Jesus, your Lord and Savior, awaits you to petition him to teach you, lead you, guide and protect you. Go to the throne room in boldness, sister, go now. Do not hesitate. The lover of your soul awaits you.

"'You will seek me and find me when you seek me with all your heart. I will be found by you,' declares the LORD, 'and will bring you back from captivity'" (Jer. 29:13–14).

The Privilege of Struggle

Featuring Condoleezza Rice

"Struggle and sorrow are not license to give way to self-doubt, self-pity, and defeat but are an opportunity to find a renewed spirit and strength to carry on."

Condoleezza Rice

ONE OF THE STRONGEST ties in the tapestry of life is with one's parents. After all, the unique combination of *them* made *you*. So, when one or both die, it's only natural to feel as though a part of your identity has been cut away or become loosely knitted together.

For Condoleezza Rice, the death of her parents would devastate her and prove to be one of the few things in life that she couldn't address with intellect or secular education.

"Terror and tragedy," she would say after 9-11, "make us more aware of our vulnerabilities and mortality." Such was the case personally for Condoleezza, when she lost her mother to cancer, then her father seven years later to a severe attack of arrhythmia. The tragedy of their deaths challenged her own faith and humanity in an unexpected way.

Both of Condoleezza's parents, John and Angelena Rice, were educators and active in their daughter's life. They went out of their way to provide her with cultural advantages as a new era of civil rights was dawning. She was raised in a tight-knit Christian family and was taught classical piano by her grandmother, then her mother, who was a musician and high school teacher.

Her father was a second-generation minister at Westminster Presbyterian Church and later the assistant vice chancellor of Denver University. He planted early seeds of determination and perseverance in a young Condoleezza's heart through biblical stories about the Israelites and of his forefathers, black slaves who fought for the freedom Condoleezza was enjoying as a child. One of the most instrumental lessons he taught Condoleezza was to learn to fight with her mind, as opposed to the examples of physical force she saw in the streets of segregated Birmingham, Alabama, where they lived.

Raised in the turbulent South during the 1960s, Condoleezza was given multiple opportunities to implement her parents' philosophies about hard work, faith, and education. Few would disagree that she succeeded. In 1989 she became the highest-ranking African-American woman ever on the National Security Counsel under George H. W. Bush's administration; and only four years later, in 1993, she became the youngest and first black female to be provost at Stanford University. Additionally, she served as the first woman to hold the position as National Security Advisor for the George W. Bush administration, and Secretary of State in the second.

"Though Birmingham had its limits," Condoleezza remembers, "my parents told me that Birmingham's limits were not mine."

To this day, Condoleezza speaks with a strong reverence about her parents and is supremely grateful to them for the morals and principles by which she was reared.

"My parents were strategic in their goals for me to rise to the top. I was going to be so well prepared, and I was going to do all of these things that were valued in white society so well that I would be armored somehow from racism. I would be able to confront white society on its own terms." And such has been the case.

Condoleezza has a long list of accolades and has worked her way into the upper echelons of a predominately white, male government. An overachiever from early childhood, Condoleezza has, by all accounts, demonstrated complete control of her life. But reality set in for her when she realized that no matter how much she studied or disciplined herself there was nothing she could do but turn to God in grief when she lost her mother in 1985, and her father on Christmas Eve seven years later.

For Condi, as she prefers to be called, the loss of her mother meant the loss of the person whose advice she valued most in the world, her source of encouragement, her refuge, her best friend and spiritual mentor. When she was age five, at her mother's request, Condi began to accompany her to the organ bench during worship services. Her mother's love for the Lord and music would be firmly planted in her heart and bring forth fruit long after her mother's death.

Her father's death left her an adult orphan with parental direction, guidance, and security permanently removed. The death of her parents stole the two people who cared for her unlike anyone else ever could and inevitably brought loss of ties to her childhood. But their deaths were not in vain. The lessons they planted in Condi's life would not go unheeded. To John Rice, God and education were the keys to overcoming obstacles, and before he died, he would be sure he impressed both onto his daughter's heart. Despite the ongoing bombings in Birmingham and the prejudice that rocked the city, he adamantly told Condi that she was a child of God, and therefore her identity was in him, not the definition the KKK or other people of prejudice proclaimed. The esteem he instilled would eventually prove to be instrumental in her ability to overcome difficulties, specifically her parents' deaths.

Among the many gifts Condoleezza's dad gave her was his own example of persevering in sorrow while clinging to the God he loved. Even as he lay dying, requiring twenty-four-hour care, he remained focused on God, sharing about his faithfulness and promises.

This is Condoleezza's story of losing her parents, and "the privilege of struggle" as she calls the time that followed.

"I was born in 1954, ten years before the Civil Rights Act was passed, in Birmingham, Alabama. I grew up in the church, never having doubts about my faith. I can honestly say, without exaggeration, that not a single day of my life have I doubted the existence of God. For someone who went to college in the early seventies, that is a bit of a remarkable statement, because it was in the sixties that *Time* magazine had a cover that remains stark in my mind. It asked, 'Is God Dead?' For me, that was never a question, especially in my home.

"My parents and I were always close. I was their only child and their constant companion, a role they took seriously. They invested time, faith, knowledge, love, and passion into my life. When I learned to play the piano at three and a half years of age, the first song I learned was 'What a Friend We Have in Jesus.' My grandmother taught me that song because she and my grandfather were people of faith, and, like my parents, wanted me to have a firm foundation in Christ. That night, after I spent eight hours learning the song, I played it for my parents. The following weekend they went out and rented a piano for me to learn on. They believed in me.

"Part of the foundation of my upbringing was a mutual respect between my parents and me, evident in the freedom to ask and engage in questions all the time. Since my father was a Presbyterian minister and my mother a woman of faith, questions always came up centered around the Bible, specifically, historical Jesus. So I grew up asking questions and getting sound answers.

"When I found out that my mother first had cancer when I was fifteen, I found myself asking an endless amount of questions that, for the first time in my life, no one had pat answers for. When my father was alive, he told me that when the results of my mother's first surgery came back, he got down on his knees and prayed, 'Lord, how am I going to raise a fifteen-year-old girl alone?' The Lord answered that prayer, and my mother lived until I was thirty. I was blessed that she was able to see me finish college and teach at Stanford. The summer before her death, I won the Walter J. Gores Award for Excellence in Teaching, and both my parents were able to attend and see me receive it in person. What a blessing those fifteen years were.

"But during those years, I had feared her death in the abstract every waking day. People who have cancer, and families who live in the shadow of terminal illness, clearly understand my fear. I could not fathom how I would survive her death. I tried to imagine life without her. What was I going to do? What would replace our nightly telephone calls? How could I ever survive Christmas or a birthday without my mother there? She was only sixty-one years old, and no intellect could soothe the hurt that was there.

"I knew that I would not be able to move beyond her death because of my intellect, and certainly not by the power of reason. Instead, I would have to trust God's Word, press in closer to him, and rest in the peace that surpasses all understanding. Only my faith in God could bridge the gap between what I was feeling and what I needed to do in dealing with my grief. I was blessed to have had seeds of faith planted in my soul about God's faithfulness from my childhood to fall back on.

"One example was when I was about twelve years old. My parents and I were visiting my grandmother's house in Birmingham, Alabama, when my mother's youngest brother, Alto, became ill in the middle of the night. The house was in complete chaos as my parents and my aunt rushed frantically to get him to the hospital. I looked around the house, and there was my grandmother just sitting on the bed, arms folded. And I said, 'Grandmother, aren't you worried about Alto?' She said, 'God's will be done.' That was it: four simple but profound words. Those words struck a chord in my heart that has resonated ever since. How many of us say that without meaning it? We repeat it again and again in the Lord's Prayer, but we don't walk in it, becoming chaotic when difficult circumstances arise.

"Another seed was planted in 1993, shortly after I was appointed provost at Stanford University. It was the story about how the university originated. Stanford University was founded out of the grief and anguish of two incredible people: Senator Leland Stanford and his wife, Jane. Their son, Leland Stanford Jr., died at the age of fifteen while traveling in Europe. At that time the Senator and Mrs. Stanford, having lost their only child, decided in their pain that they would do something good for other people's children, so they started the university. It went on to be a successful college, indeed helping to educate thousands of young adults.

"Years later, when Senator Stanford died, the university was, in a real sense, founded a second time. After he passed on, the university faced a dire financial crisis that almost led to its closure. The senator had paid all of the university's expenses personally over the years, and after his death the United States government seized his assets in a dispute over his railroad. The university was suddenly penniless. Jane Stanford's advisors told her that her only choice was to close the university. Instead, she rejected that advice and reduced her personal staff from seventeen to three, kept $350 a month out of the $10,000 permitted her by the courts, and placed the faculty on her personal payroll. Over the years thousands of individuals have been able to attain their education because of the sacrifice of these two people in the midst of their personal heartache.

"As I reflect on those acts of faith and courage, first, at the original founding of the university after the death of their son Leland, then again after Senator Stanford died, I realize that Senator and Mrs. Stanford were testament to a belief that we have all but lost in modern life—the conviction that struggle and sorrow are not a license to give way to self-doubt, self-pity and defeat but rather an opportunity to find a renewed spirit and strength to carry on. Those acts of self-sacrifice in the midst of heartache are perfect examples that today's defeat can be turned into tomorrow's victory.

"As much as we hate to admit it, few of us would have made the same decisions. We live in a world of instant gratification. Our self-centeredness and underlying search for that which makes us feel good today, at whatever the expense and cost tomorrow, is spiritually self-mutilating. Although Christians know that our earthly lives are not yet the final act, we too behave as the ancient Euripideans did, living foolishly for today because tomorrow we might die.

"I learned three important truths while grieving the loss of my parents that I would like to share with you as you grapple with your own grief. First, I feel impressed to tell you that it is a privilege to struggle. Only through struggle do we realize the depth of our resilience and understand that the hardest of blows can be survived. Through struggle we learn to let go of fear and strive for freedom. Only in struggle do we attain the knowledge that, like a house of cards, the human spirit is fragile and human strength fleeting.

"As believers, we can take unique advantage of this truth because in times of despair we can seek a closer relationship with our Lord. How else are we to get to know the full measure of the Lord's capacity for intervention in our lives? If there are no burdens, how can we know that he will be there to lift them?

"It is easy to thank God when all is going well. It is much harder to trust him in times of trial. I think that this is an especially hard lesson, an especially hard belief for those of us who have relied on education, intellect, and reason to guide us. We get sidetracked sometimes and begin to believe that our own wisdom guides us. The media doesn't help. Every single day they bombard us with messages that tell us we can only believe that which we can prove.

"I have had to live my life in the world of the mind because of my career choices. I spend every waking day dedicated to the search to know truth. I am surrounded in my life by standards of evidence and methods of proof. It is sometimes hard to accept the simple faith required to trust in God opposed to my own wisdom.

"The Lord gave us a brain, and I'm quite sure that he expects us to use it, though I'm sure he must be mightily disappointed sometimes. In doing so, there will be times that we wrestle with our faith, questioning and trying to understand God. I have never believed that God intended us to leave the powers of reason aside when we encounter questions of theology, seeming contradictions in our belief, or even when we have questions to ask him. But there are times when intellect and reason fail, when the burden is just too heavy, when it just makes no sense. Those are moments in life that we can't explain what's happening to us and we must turn to God to be comforted.

"Church, God, and Christianity were like breathing in my family. And while I grew up being certain in my religious faith, it is easy for me to go on spiritual autopilot. If I'm not careful, my faith in Christ can become as habitual as putting on a sweater or eating breakfast in the morning. As a response, my intellect often gets in the way of my faith.

"A couple of years ago I attended the memorial service for a nineteen-year-old Stanford student who was killed in a car accident. I was struck by the fact that the mourners who attended her memorial were so young. It should be decades before they have to go to a funeral for one of their peers. It makes no sense to ask why. There aren't any answers. At those times the relationship that we have developed with God, having trusted him in times of struggle is the key to our survival. That is when it is time just to give up and turn to God. That is when it is time to let go and take everything to God in prayer. We have a reliable friend to help us through, one who sticks closer than a brother.

"The apostle Paul affirmed this more beautifully than any before him or any since. Locked in prison, Paul warned off those who would feel sorry for him. To the Philippians, Paul wrote, 'I have learned in whatever state I am, to be content. I know how to be abased, and I know how to abound. Everywhere and in all things I have learned both to be full and to be hungry, both to abound and to suffer need' (Phil. 4:11–12 NKJV). As Paul taught in this brilliant passage, finding peace in the midst of pain is the fulfillment of one's humility, and the relationship with God is complete.

"There's a second truth about struggle: it can conquer you, or you can conquer it. We are all in a constant search of heroes. This is because they are people who remind us that we can beat the odds. Whether it's Joe Montana helping bring a team back from insurmountable odds as he did multiple times in his career, or Dan Jansen, the speed skater in the Winter Olympics who disappointed America twice in Olympic competition and still found the will to train four more years and ultimately to win a gold medal, we keep looking for people who can show us how to triumph over what may appear to be insurmountable circumstances. When other people rise above their circumstances, we feel empowered to do the same. The core attitude of a hero is found in the way that they meet life's challenges.

"Among my heroes are my grandfathers. Both were excellent examples of how not to allow difficult circumstances to overcome you but instead to overcome your circumstances. My Granddaddy Ray ran away from home at the age of thirteen with nothing but a railroad token in his pocket. He worked two jobs during the week as a mining contractor and blacksmith, and on Saturdays, he built houses. In the deepest, darkest segregated part of Birmingham, he and my grandmother put all five of their children through college. And thus, my future was assured.

"My other grandfather, Grandpa Rice, was a poor farmer's son in Utah, Alabama. One day, he decided he needed to get 'book learning.' He asked someone passing by, 'Where can a colored man go to school?' They said that there was a little Presbyterian school not too far away called Stillman College, a school where my father would later serve as dean. So my Grandpa Rice saved up his cotton to pay for his education, and he took off for Tuscaloosa some forty miles away. But when he got there, he realized that he couldn't pay for his tuition with cotton. He needed money. So he questioned how the other boys were going to college and was told they were on scholarship. Then they told him that if he wanted to be a Presbyterian minister, he could have a scholarship too. My grandfather said, 'That's actually just what I had in mind.' And that was how my grandfather became a Presbyterian minister. He got his degree in 1920 or so, and because of his determination and perseverance, I am the daughter, the granddaughter, and the niece of Presbyterian ministers.

"Part of not allowing struggle to overcome your faith is attained by letting go of our own expectations and plans. Women are used to handling households, raising children, meeting the needs of their mate, and often while working full-time outside the home. Things generally run smoothly for women when they control the circumstances around them. They've set the schedule and the time line for the events that occur from meals to homework to transportation. They are experts at listening and figuring out the cues of the people in their life and moving them in the direction needed to accomplish the goals of the family.

"Women are used to handling difficult circumstances daily in a methodic, calculated manner. It takes a lot of faith to step back from that approach and let go when we need to grieve or work through any type of struggle. After my parents' deaths I was challenged with such a circumstance.

"I had gone to the doctor for a checkup when, during my breast exam, my doctor found something unusual. My mother died from breast cancer, so this was not good news. My doctor said something like, 'Well, don't worry, it's early. Whatever it is, it's early.' Believe me, I was less worried about how early it was than what it was. But the doctor said he didn't know and wouldn't know for about a week. That was one of the longest seven-day periods of my life.

"During the first few days after meeting with my doctor, I found myself planning my future. How was this illness going to interfere with my life? How was I going to keep working if I had cancer? I started planning whom I would tell and whom I wouldn't. I had a schedule all laid out *if* indeed I did have breast cancer. One night toward the end of my seven-day waiting period, I woke up in the wee hours of the morning and thought, *Have you lost your mind?* I realized that I was attempting to control a circumstance that I had no control over. So I changed the way I had been praying.

"I started by asking God to take control of the situation. That meant that I had to let go of it. Additionally, I began to ask him how this experience could teach me about what I really should be doing with my life and to show me what I wasn't getting done in my life. I made the radical break between faith and reason, letting go of my expectations and plans and allowing God to take them. I thank the Lord that I didn't end up having cancer but was also thankful for the lesson I learned in the process of finding out.

"Next I realized the importance of taking the time to grapple with my circumstance in his presence. I needed time for silence, reflection, and meditation. I had to make time to sit and be still so that I could hear the still, small voice of calm that doesn't come when I'm allowing my intellect and reason to dominate every waking moment.

"There is a third truth in the privilege of struggle. You can find personal fulfillment and peace in times of pain and heartache. Difficulties are necessary to hone the spirit and to make us aware of the power not only to survive but to overcome. It is an even greater gift to be able to turn one's sorrow to the good and benefit of others.

"Consider again Jane Stanford, the powerful woman of God, who, when her faith was tested and purified with the death of her son, and then later, her husband. She is later quoted as saying:

> My dear husband was suddenly and unexpectedly called from earth to the fair beyond. For a while, I felt like one on a sinking ship on a tempestuous sea. I shuttered and closed my eyes as I thought the ship would sink but clung to God's promises to the helpless, the widow, the weary who wanted rest. I wanted to join my loved ones and was not afraid to die. Suddenly, there loomed out before me, the blessed work left to my care by my loved ones, and I felt that my course was cowardly. I promised most solemnly to live for the work that I now saw was God's work, not mine. I promised most solemnly to live for that work and to do my best.

"I've often wondered if Mrs. Stanford's decision to somehow sustain Stanford University was a decision of a grieving widow and mother who wanted to continue to immortalize her son and her husband. But it is clear to me from her response that she in fact saw a higher calling. She understood the link between her own pain and suffering and her calling to God.

"Few of us are presented with so many dramatic opportunities to demonstrate that struggle can be for the good. But there are times in our lives when we are called to rise above our pain and to help others. In today's society every person, group, and state seems determined to dwell on that which has not been given to us and to point constantly to that which has been given to others. Nothing good is borne of personal struggle if it is used to fuel one's sense of entitlement or superiority to those who, in our own perception, have struggled less. It is a dangerous thing to ask why you have been given less than someone. It is humbling and healthy to ask why you have been given so much.

"Struggle is not to be worn as a badge of honor. Perhaps this is why in describing his personal struggle, the apostle Paul felt it necessary to say to the Philippians, 'Forgetting those things which are behind and reaching forward to those things which are ahead, I press toward the goal for the prize of the upward call of God in Jesus Christ' (Phil. 3:13–14 NKJV). Struggle can only be turned to the good of others if we can let go of the pain, bad memories, and the sense of unfairness of the, 'Why me,' that inevitably accompanies personal turmoil.

"We as Christians need to reaffirm for our troubled world that struggle is a privilege. The human condition contains one central paradox, one that philosophers, religious leaders, and people of letters have tried to explain throughout the centuries. It is a lesson that is at the root of Christianity, at the basis of our belief in the resurrection. It was revealed to us at the founding of our faith in the most dramatic way possible. It is that our Lord Jesus Christ suffered a horrible death only to rise again. There was Good Friday, but there was also Easter Sunday.

"The paradox of the human condition then is this: in death we find life; in turmoil we find peace; one must lose one's life to gain it; and in struggle we find that which is irrepressible in the human spirit, and always there in our relationship with God. The affirmation of that paradox of the human condition, a belief in the privilege of struggle, is heard in the words of a Negro spiritual.

"In the most horrendous of conditions, when it must have seemed that there was no way out, nowhere to go, slaves raised their voices in the song 'Nobody Knows the Trouble I've Seen.' From the depth of their pain, they knew that although others may not understand their heartache, Jesus did. As they sang, 'Nobody knows the trouble I've seen; nobody knows but Jesus. Nobody knows the trouble I've seen, Glory Hallelujah. Sometimes I'm up, sometimes I'm down, yes Lord, You know sometimes I'm almost to the ground. Nobody knows the trouble I've seen, nobody knows but Jesus,' they knew they spoke from the power of the resurrection.

"I often wonder how completely the church understands suffering and the context of joyful, hand clapping, dancing that is found in black gospel. Gospel was born in the small, hot, black churches where the people who were celebrating, were oddly enough, those who had nothing to celebrate in this earthly life. The joyful celebration came from the depths of despair. The church was the one place they could express joy. Black gospel is directly tied to the pain and suffering that was the legacy of slavery and segregation. The context needs to be understood, that there is a link between joy and pain, faith and perseverance, and struggle and salvation.

"Again the words of the apostle Paul are relevant: 'I was given a painful wound to my pride, which came as Satan's messenger to bruise me. Three times I begged God to rid me of it, but God's answer was: "My grace is sufficient for you, for my power is made perfect in weakness" (2 Cor. 12:7–10). Therefore I shall prefer to find my joy and my pride in the things that are my weakness; and then the power of Christ will come and rest upon me. For this reason I am content, for the sake of Christ, with weakness, contempt, persecution, hardship, and frustration; for when I am weak, then I am strong.'

"Once again, it is a privilege to struggle. When God's power is full strength because we are weak, that enables the Spirit of the Lord to rest on us, it is indeed a great day in the Lord. When, for the sake of Christ, we are weak, contemptible, persecuted, frustrated, and painfully grieving, and because we are weak, he is strong, it is a blessed day in the Lord.

"As Christians, we sometimes take for granted God's intricate plan for our lives. I have had my struggles, as perhaps you have, but frankly, when I look at what other people have confronted on a daily basis, like what my parents and grandparents dealt with, I am reminded that I have hardly lived the life of Job. And with that grace and support from God I have come to terms with every day.

"Only through struggle can we realize the depth of our resilience and understand that in the darkest of nights we can let go of fear and rest in the freedom of the shadow of the Lord who suffered all things for us. It is only through struggle that we can truly understand the truth in rejoicing in suffering, found in Romans 5:3, 'Not only so, but we also rejoice in our sufferings, because we know that suffering produces perseverance.'"

Living with Regrets

Featuring First Lady Laura Bush

"I grieved a lot. It was a horrible, horrible tragedy.
It's a terrible feeling to be responsible for an accident. . . .
It was a sign of the preciousness of life and how fleeting it can be."

Laura Bush, *O Magazine*

SHE IS PEACEFULLY CALM with a graceful but forceful demeanor, soft-spoken yet forthright, reserved but conscientiously polite with a witty sense of humor. Perhaps her most notable distinction is her commitment to her daughters and her grave concern and compassion for those she loves, particularly her husband. These honed characteristics were hard won for the first lady from Midland, Texas, but are a profound proclamation of God's grace as told in Romans 8:28, "And we know that in all things God works for the good of those who love him, who have been called according to his purpose."

Laura Bush was called by God but not without criticism from man. When her husband was running for the presidency, the media exposed a tragedy and death caused by Laura Welch when she was seventeen years old. Attacks against her character and integrity bombarded her husband's run for office from every angle. But Laura remained calm and confident, standing against the accusatory slander knowing that tragedies can be overcome through prayer and faith.

Raised in the oil-rich dust bowl of west Texas, Laura Welch was an only child to Harold Welch, an ambitious and sociable man, and Jenna Welch, one of seven girls raised on a successful dairy farm by a prematurely widowed mother. Although Jenna is fondly remembered by her daughter as an affectionate mother, it was the love, care, and sense of humor of both parents that shaped the formative years of the first lady.

"I was blessed to have a solid, affectionate mother and a father with a roaring sense of humor. Additionally, I was sheltered by the freedom of living in a small town in a way I didn't understand at the time."

Laura was raised on Humble Avenue in Midland, Texas, a small town embodied by dozens of churches during the time of the growing oil industry. She was surrounded by strong women including, but not limited to, her mother and grandmother. She learned early in life that women had a place in the world and later would be quoted as saying, "I've always done what really traditional women do, and I've been very, very satisfied."

Laura was innocent about life outside of Midland, and the safety of the small town inspired her to participate in the many opportunities offered her through local organizations. As a young girl Laura was involved in Brownie Scouts, the church choir, ballet, swimming lessons, and the Honor Society. She also loved to practice being a teacher, an aspiration she held for many years that would eventually come into fruition.

As a teen Laura Welch enjoyed an active social life. She enjoyed spending time with friends at a local teen hangout called Agnes' Drive-in. She was well liked and kept busy as a member of the yearbook staff and a student in several honors classes.

During her high school years Laura participated in an event that gave her and other young ladies of Lee High School an excuse to rough it up on the football field; they played in a powder-puff football game against their rival, Midland High School. The game involved role reversals for the students, with the girls donning football jerseys and the boys dressing in cheerleader outfits. Laura was among those girls who wore a football uniform and ran out onto the football field to play.

During one of these powder-puff games in her junior year, Laura met a young man who would later play a defining role in her life—Michael Douglas. Dark haired and athletic, Douglas was both a track star and a member of the football team. Mike was one of the pom-pom waving powder-puff cheerleaders during the powder-puff game and almost instantly fell for Laura.

Michael excelled at practically everything he attempted, and he made friends easily. By the time he entered Lee High School, the same year as Laura, Mike was already one of Midland's most popular boys. Described by friends as being both nice looking and witty, Mike had a unique quality and gregarious personality that drew people to him. Mike and Laura began dating, and by the spring they had become one of Lee High School's most noticeable couples.

The summer before her senior year, Laura worked as a counselor at Camp Mystic, eighty miles northwest of San Antonio on the Guadalupe River. Here Laura had the opportunity to work with children and earn money for her senior year. Always full of fun and enthusiasm, Laura was especially liked by the kids at camp, and for the first time she began to envision an exciting future before her. It seemed as if nothing could go wrong.

Things had cooled off between Laura and Mike over the summer while she worked at the camp, and Mike had since become seriously involved with one of Laura's friends. Laura and Mike remained friends, and after a particularly fierce game between Lee and San Angelo High, she looked on proudly as Mike was presented with a sportsmanship trophy. Still the perfect couple in the eyes of their peers, the pair were among the favorites to be chosen homecoming king and queen.

Laura plunged into her senior year with even more gusto than usual. She joined the yearbook staff, the student council, and the 100 Club. Laura's future held great promise.

On Laura's seventeenth birthday, her parents hosted a small party for their teenage daughter. Two days later Laura asked her father if she could borrow the family car to drive to a friend's party. Even though it was a Wednesday, Laura's parents did not hesitate to hand her the keys to their sedan. "Don't worry," she told them. "I promise I'll be home by ten."

Laura picked up her friend Judy. It was a dry, clear, cool night as their car sped just north of town. The girls laughed and chatted. As was the custom in Texas in 1963, Laura was not wearing a seat belt.

Laura and Judy were deep in conversation as they barreled north on Farm Road 868. The speed limit on the outskirts of town was sixty-five miles per hour; Laura was going fifty. Neither girl could remember exactly what they were talking about when Laura failed to notice the stop sign that stood in plain, unobstructed view at the intersection of Farm Road 868 and State Road 349. It was particularly important that she see the sign, for this was a two-way stop; there was no stop sign for cross traffic.

Laura had no idea what was about to happen when, at 8:08 p.m., she ran the stop sign and plowed into the side of a car traveling east on State Road 349. But she would never forget the horrific, deafening sound of the two cars colliding. Glass shattered everywhere, tires burned in an attempt to stop the vehicle, and steel crunched like a pop can around them. Laura quickly lost control of her car. The two girls screamed as they lurched forward on impact, then slid across the highway and into a shallow ditch.

The sole occupant of the other car wouldn't know what hit him. Struck on the right front passenger side, the driver's car slid, turned, and veered off the pavement in what seemed like an instant. Even before the car came to rest in a cloud of dust, its driver was dead. As a result of the violent impact, the young man's neck snapped, and he was thrown from the car.

Seconds later the young man's father came upon the scene; he happened to be following his son in another car, and he witnessed the crash. He held his son's head in his hands and wept inconsolably as police and ambulance personnel lifted the seventeen-year-old's lifeless body onto a stretcher. The victim was taken to Midland Memorial Hospital, where he was later pronounced dead on arrival. His father, who witnessed his own son's death, would suffer from an onslaught of nightmares for the rest of his life.

Miraculously, Laura and her friend Judy suffered only a few scratches and bruises. A second ambulance took the girls to the same hospital, where Laura's parents were summoned to meet them. It was then that her parents learned that Laura had plowed through a stop sign and T-boned into a car with the right-of-way. Her parents were assured that Laura and her high school friend Judy Dykes were fine aside from a few bruises and being upset, but the boy in the other car had died from the force of the broadside impact.

"It hurt all of us deeply," Jenna Welch recalled. "Laura is an only child. It was dreadful to think she might have been killed."

Laura and Judy had been too shaken up to pay much attention to the other car, but now they inquired about the driver. Laura was told he had died. She was crushed by the news and broke down in the emergency room. Yet she still didn't know the identity of the driver who was killed.

Hospital personnel didn't tell Laura that the young man in the other car was her friend Mike Douglas. The heartbreaking task of telling Laura fell to her parents. Later, when they broke the news, she was devastated.

Released from the hospital that night, Laura returned home and isolated herself from the reality of the tragedy in her room, unable to return to school or even talk to friends. The pain and loss of losing Mike had taken the heart and life out of her.

The following morning the front-page article in the *Midland Reporter-Telegram* told the facts of the tragedy as if it were just another accident. "Police said death was attributed to a broken neck," and "Lee High School Senior Dies in Traffic Mishap." It was far from accusatory, but the small-town gossip line reeled with Laura's name as the one who had caused the death.

The reality of the incident was tragic and unforgiving, leaving the teenage Laura shattered. Neither Laura nor her parents attended the memorial service the following Saturday. Laura was still badly shaken and worried that Michael's parents would resent her if she showed up at the funeral. "Won't they hate me?" she asked her mother. "I killed their son."

The accident changed Laura forever. Years later she still describes it as "crushing." "Crushing for the family involved and for me as well," she says. The accident forced her to see that life has just as much tragedy as joy. As a response, Laura became more reserved and less gregarious, more understanding, and less judgmental toward others.

When she was not in her room crying inconsolably, Laura sought counseling from her pastor at First Methodist as she tried to grapple with this loss and her sense of guilt. "I grieved a lot," she explains decades later. "It was a horrible, horrible tragedy. It's a terrible feeling to be responsible for an accident. And it was horrible for all of us to lose him, especially since he was so young. But at some point I had to accept that death is a part of life, and as tragic as losing Mike was, there was nothing anyone could do to change that."

Friends say that Mike's parents went out of their way to make clear that they did not blame Laura for their son's death, but for Laura it was a relentless memory that reminded her of a fatal mistake she'd made.

Mike's death left his classmates stunned into silence, so when Laura finally returned to school, she too remained silent about the tragedy. But as a result, Laura dropped out of a number of student activities. She did choose, however, to remain on the yearbook staff. She wanted to help write a full-page tribute to the boy whose life she had cut short.

"I can still see those eyes—full of delight," Laura wrote. "The mouth—ever a smile. An armload of books on one hip, and the walk that so resembled youthful confidence." The poem went on to praise Douglas's "sense of fun, the effervescent good will, the sportsmanship, and the obedience to duty." In a touching final verse, Laura and her friends mused, "His imprint lingers in the halls, where he walked only a while ago. So I'll close my eyes. And remember. And I'll smile." The memorial in the yearbook expresses solemn respect for the boy who lost his life that Midland evening, but for Laura it was a memory that she'd never be able to forget.

Concern for Laura continued for the year to come as she attended her senior year. "Just look in Laura's eyes," one friend noted. "The pain is right there. She has never gotten away from it, not entirely. And she never will. It still haunts her. . . . She is a very controlled person; she has to be. Otherwise she'd just crumble."

In a television biography about Laura, Midland resident Jack Hickman shared the heartache that encompassed the hearts of those who lived in the small town. "It was as if two of Midland's favorites had been involved in an unthinkable act of fate."

Laura's parents could do nothing to help their daughter's pain subside, but their close relationship with her helped her heal over time. They were a solid, down-to-earth Christian family, and the accident caused Laura to become reflective and look for strength outside of herself and friends and family. She found that strength in her faith, something that would be called upon again, in future years, not only during other personal strains and setbacks but also during times of triumph.

The same faith in God that Laura turned to at seventeen became instrumental in President Bush's life during their first years of marriage. A self-proclaimed alcoholic, George W. Bush was a Texas "bad boy." Not long after their marriage, Laura encouraged him to join her at her Methodist church. Soon he was teaching Sunday school at First Methodist in Midland and serving on several church committees. Later she took him to a James Dobson seminar in hopes of seeing him grow in his spiritual walk. During his drinking years she stood by him, encouraging him to stop. By her example, prayer, and through perseverance, her husband's heart softened, and he became passionate about his own identity in Christ. Now he says, "You know, I had a drinking problem. Right now I should be in a bar in Texas, not the Oval Office. There is only one reason that I am in the Oval Office and not in a bar. I found faith. I found God. I am here because of the power of prayer."[1]

Critics of the first lady said that 9-11 would be a test of her faith and of her ability to remain calm, but the test of faith was at seventeen. What we see now is the result of years of faith in Christ. Even now, as a woman's advocate and the wife of our nation's president, she is not shy about her faith in God and takes opportunity after opportunity to share her beliefs

In a recent *New York Times* interview, Laura stated that her favorite book was *The Brothers Karamazov* by Feodor Dostoyevsky, and that her favorite part of the book was "The Legend of the Grand Inquisitor," which addresses the fundamental Christian struggle between following the rules and regulations of organized religion and developing the strength to follow the true path of Christ, a path of absolute freedom. Such is the proclamation of her own life—one of freedom as she walks in integrity, wisdom, and strength. But such boldness in sharing her faith is not uncommon. She continually professes her belief in the value and worth of every human being as a child of God. She has referenced that children should be taught in not only schools but also through churches and

Sunday schools, continually referencing the importance of Christ in one's life.

Additionally, during the tragedy of 9-11, Laura Bush was praised for her reassuring manner and the support of her husband after the terrorist attacks. She found her composure and stood solidly by the man she loves. Where did such integrity come from?

"Causing Mike Douglas's death made me have more of a perspective on life. And maybe I would already have had that perspective anyway. I just got it at seventeen," she says.

Since the tragedy of 9-11, Laura has focused her energy on helping our nation, especially children, through the healing process—something she is familiar with herself. She has personally comforted many victims and families of victims of the terrorist attacks. She has written letters to others who are grieving and has attended many memorial and prayer services.

The compassion, perseverance, and faith she learned as a teen have now touched the lives of millions. Who would have ever thought that a teenager involved in a tragedy that took the life of another would be used as a vessel in the hand of God for not just her family but for a nation?

From Prejudice to Prominence

Featuring Kay Coles James

"For the first month, I never made it from one class to the next without at least one student pricking me with a pin. Sometimes I was stuck so many times I had to press my dress against my body to keep the red streams from dripping down my legs."

Kay Coles James

WHEN ROSA PARKS refused to give up her seat on a Montgomery, Alabama, bus in 1955, her silent defiance spoke for a race of individuals long oppressed. Rosa's actions would pave the way for freedom for African-Americans in ways yet unseen but not without a price. Many blacks suffered (and are still suffering), at the hands of racists who would torture, kill, and punish those who stood up for their God-given right to be treated like a human being. Rosa did not know that there was a six-year-old in Portsmouth, Virginia, during that same time who would be directly affected by her stand. Her actions that day would pave the way for this little girl to rise up out of poverty and prejudice and go on to become one of the most influential women in American history.

In the hot summer month of June 1949, Madeline Kay Coles was brought into the world on the kitchen table of her family's apartment. The fifth of six children born into a family struggling with an alcoholic father and a mother forced to rely on welfare, all odds were against her. To further complicate things, Kay was born in an era when blacks and whites were segregated. Blacks were denied the right to ride at the front of a bus, attend white schools, or use the public libraries.

Kay was raised in a humble house with linoleum floors and peeling, painted walls. Her neighborhood was a series of small, two-bedroom houses that had been army barracks during the war. As the only girl, she shared a bedroom with her parents, and her five brothers shared the other one. Her father, who worked as a longshoreman at the nearby navy yard, was adamant about two things—providing for his family and drinking whiskey. When providing for his family was cut short by lack of work, his failure and inability to provide turned into vicious tirades of verbal and physical abuse.

Her mother, a simple woman from a prominent family, had shocked and disappointed her parents when she had dropped out of college to marry, especially since she didn't "have to." The black sheep of the family, Kay's mother wore the proverbial cloak of disgrace her parents clothed her in with dignity, despite her husband's addiction and abuse, and committed herself to raising her children unto the Lord.

"I knew that I could count on greens at Sunday dinner, baths on Saturday night, and Mama always taking the six of us kids to church on Sundays," Kay says now. "Each night before bed Mama required us to get on our knees to say our prayers. Once when the cold of winter seeped through the wooden floor, one of my brothers complained about this ritual. Mama quickly cut him off. She said, 'Son, you get on your feet to play football, you crouch in the bushes to play tag, you can sure enough get on your knees to pray to your God!'"

During her childhood Kay remembers moving several times when her father was out of work, living with relatives and barely making a living.

"We moved in with my great-great-aunt Duk in a rickety Victorian home. During the cold winter months, we could see our breath as we whispered good-nights into the air. During that season Mama would pile coats, clothes, and old towels on top of us to help keep us warm as we lay in bed. None of us minded being doubled and tripled up in bed then. The more bodies the warmer—and the better."

But the battle warring in her father's soul would eventually be won by the whiskey, and Kay's mother would have to move into public housing in order to raise her six children without fear and alcoholism.

"My first impression of the projects was of pleasant-looking buildings surrounded by grass and playgrounds. Once inside however, it lost all of its humanity. Although the gray cinderblock walls and dreary concrete floor were hard to cope with, the worst adjustment was the hundreds and hundreds of cockroaches!"

Winter nights were spent doubled and tripled up in bed again with her brothers. And although times were tough, Kay relished in the safety, warmth, and love she felt from her mother and brothers.

"Lord, bless the children who don't have anyone to sleep with to keep them warm at night," she'd whisper as she closed her eyes to sleep.

Because she lived in subsidized housing, Kay was referred to as a "project nigger" by the white people and even some blacks who lived on the "hill," the more affluent black neighborhood.

"I may have been hungry and poor, but I was neat-and-clean hungry and poor," Kay says. "My mother always made sure her children were well mannered and presentable."

Hatred for blacks was intensifying as they began to fight for freedom from the bondage of segregation. In a field not even a half mile from her home where she and her siblings sometimes played football, the KKK would hold cross burnings.

"It used to scare me to death when cars filled with yoo-hooing hooded whites drove down Nine Mile Road, headed for the big rally. It never was clear in my mind that they hated us because we were black. I didn't understand racism. I just knew that they were evil people who would hurt a little girl if she was caught alone near the field on a rally night."

But the unmarked boundaries between whites and blacks were clearly drawn. Kay and her brothers were never to cross Nine Mile Road, the busy two-lane street that passed in front of the project housing, that stood as the only "gray" area that separated the poor and needy blacks from the affluent and wealthy whites.

When Kay was about six, her Aunt Pearl and Uncle J. B. began taking her to their home on a regular basis. She looked forward to these times away from the noise of her brothers and the continued flow of confusion from people coming in and out of the house. She felt like a princess during this time. Her Aunt Pearl would braid her hair, putting in new barrettes, and have her change into a new dress that she had purchased for Kay.

"Not only did I have my own room, but I even had my very own bed. It was the first time that I had ever slept in a bed without at least two of my brothers," she remembers. "Then one afternoon Mama called me into the kitchen and gave me the news. As she set me up on her lap, close to her bosom as she did on the few occasions when she did my hair, I knew that something was wrong. Her tear-swollen eyes confirmed my hunches. She said, 'Child, opportunity don't come knocking but so many times in a person's life. Your Aunt Pearl and Uncle J. B., because they love you so much and want to provide opportunities for you, they want you to live with them.'"

Kay was devastated. She resisted the thought in her heart, and tears and a muffled moan followed. Her mother knew that her aunt and uncle could give her things she could never afford, a real life with vacations, nice clothes, and the option to go to college. But Kay didn't care about those things. She wanted to stay with her mother and brothers. She shook her head defiantly in rejection and protest.

"'Kay, darling,' my Mama said, 'Little boys can play in the gutter and get up the next morning, put on a clean shirt, and nobody thinks anything of it because they're boys. A little girl can play in the gutter and get up the next morning, and everybody remembers. And I want you out of this gutter. This is an opportunity for you. I'm still your mama, and I will always be your mama, but you're going to take advantage of these opportunities. They're going to give you things that I can't give you.'"

Kay obeyed her mother, never questioning her love, but her heart ached. Out of obedience she hugged each of her brothers good-bye and climbed into her aunt and uncle's Chrysler. As it pulled away, she watched through blurry eyes as she crossed over Nine Mile Road from the projects into the privileged side of town.

It didn't take Kay long to realize, though, that prejudice wasn't something she left behind. As a matter of fact, on both sides of Nine Mile Road, despite new clothes, a bed she didn't have to share, and a home that was cockroach free, it was evident that prejudice still remained; and the invisible line between "niggers" and white folks, professionals and servants, and men and women still existed.

"There was a firm conviction among black folks that education was our avenue to freedom, so everyone took an interest in our schoolwork. This academic focus was heightened in my case because my aunt was a schoolteacher herself. Every morning I tagged along with her to attend Webster Davis, where she taught.

"At that point in my life I had so little firsthand experience with white folks that my understanding of them came almost entirely from my teachers. That was in the 1950s when there were few opportunities for educated blacks to get jobs, so while we had black teachers with Ph.D.s teaching elementary school, they also told us that white kids were given all the breaks and advantages and that we had to be better than them to be treated equally. We were told in no uncertain terms that we had to be twice as good and twice as smart to survive. 'Life is not fair,' I heard many teachers say, 'and so don't go looking for fair.' No one at Webster Davis Elementary School ever led us to believe that we could expect to get anything in life that we didn't sweat, bleed, and work for."

These lessons were reinforced in Kay's home with a religious fervor. When she came home from school, she was required to pore over her lessons hour after hour with her aunt prodding her. As her aunt drank beer, she would pore over Kay's work, checking for errors, and berating her. Her aunt was a vicious drunk, insulting her father for his lack of provision, and in turn, Kay. "You aren't going to amount to a thing!" she'd yell. "The Coles blood in you is going to ruin you! Bitch! You little Coles whore!"

"She would crumple up my math homework and screech at me that I had done them all wrong. The problems were easy enough to check in my head so I could know for sure that my answers were correct. I would redo the problems again and again, each time my aunt insisting that I was such an 'ignorant fool' that I had answered every one wrong, until eventually she would relent and say that I'd finally gotten them right."

Kay's first year of junior high was potentially racially explosive. A man had taken the school system to court, and the judge had decided that schools should be integrated. The weight of that decision to integrate weighed little on Kay's heart. She was preoccupied with what the integration meant to black students that were thrust into white territory, to learn new diction, new customs, and new ways of doing things. And she was rightly concerned about how the white folk would respond.

"Some parents were so upset by the thought of their kids sitting beside black children that they withdrew their children from public schools. We feared there might be violence. I was one of twenty-six black students joining the incoming class of three hundred white students at my junior high. I felt overwhelmed. I walked softly down the halls, my head down, intimidated.

"For the first month, I never made it from one class to the next without at least one student pricking me with a pin. Sometimes I was stuck so many times I had to press my dress against my body to keep the red streams from dripping down my legs. I tried to be discreet. I didn't want them to know that their taunts or their jabs hurt me."

Kay's greatest fear was being caught alone in the hallway with one of the many students that took joy in threatening the blacks. One day it happened.

"I was descending a large stairway when a group of white kids started up. Most of them ignored me as I tried to step down the side.

But one of them waited till my back was turned and pushed me, hard, down the stairs. I landed at the end with my shins and back bruised. Apparently it wasn't enough for him, so he kicked my books all over the hall as well. The crowd laughed and made jokes."

Then an amazing thing happened. A girl Kay had never spoken with before stepped out of the crowd and began helping her pick up her books. She continued to help Kay despite the ridicule of her friends as they accused her of being a "nigger lover."

"Unfazed, she walked me down the hall to the office. She didn't say much, but she said enough to make clear that the boy who pushed me spoke and acted for himself, not for all white people," Kay remembers. "I will never forget her act of courage."

Kay came to expect the pinpricks and name calling from the students, but she had faith that if things got really bad, blacks could turn to their teachers for support. She couldn't have been more disappointed when one day during homeroom, when, reading from the menu, the teacher said, "Today we're having grilled cheese sandwiches, vegetable soup, milk, and brownies for dessert." At that point the teacher paused and looked over her glasses at Kay and added for the class's enjoyment, "And heaven knows why they're having brownies. We have enough of them here already."

As Kay's Aunt Pearl continued drinking, her tongue-lashings continued, worsening as Kay went into high school. At times her aunt would become so angry and accusatory that she would kick Kay out of the house. These were times of confusion for Kay, as she matured, but as she was growing up, she hadn't really considered turning to the God her mother loved and had served.

"I was on familiar terms with God, having grown up accustomed to hearing my mother call upon his name almost daily, but I wasn't much of a pray-er, except when I was in trouble, and then I could be quite eloquent."

Kay's aunt and uncle went to church about four times a year. Inside the walls of the church, Kay's identity in Christ was affirmed. She learned that she was God's beloved child and created in his image.

"Knowing this made me feel like I was a valuable and cherished child. The church also taught me that hate destroys the human spirit, but love builds it up. Part of the magnetic draw of the black church was the warm fellowship. It was one of few places where 'our kind' could go to find love, acceptance, and that most scarce of all commodities, respect.

"But the older I became, however, the less sense I could make of what I heard and saw in church. I thought long and hard about the porcelain Jesus hanging limply from the cross on the wall. It often caused my little mind to question how a blue-eyed, blond Jesus could love dark, nappy me. Would there be a separate section in heaven, in the back near the edge separating heaven and hell, for us blacks?

"The whole business about being a Christian also confused me. In tightly knit communities like ours, everybody knows everybody else's business. It puzzled me that many of those who sang, professed, confessed, and preached on Sunday lived rather unchristian lives the rest of the week. By the time I entered my senior year of high school, I had pretty much decided that Christianity was a great set of rules to govern your life, but that was it. I was a good kid, I always had been, and if God graded on the curve, I'd surely get into heaven."

One evening, Kay and her aunt and uncle sat around the kitchen table, eating dinner with the television droning on in the background as it usually did during meals. The show caught her attention from across the room. Kay neglected to eat as she sat glued to the screen as if the man speaking were talking specifically to her.

"Do you feel an emptiness in your heart?" the man asked. "A lack of purpose and meaning in your life?"

Kay's heart was responsive as she listened.

"There's a place in our soul that only Jesus Christ can fill," he explained.

Kay could relate to an emptiness in her heart.

"Going to church doesn't make you a Christian any more than going to a garage makes you a car," he said.

"Then what does make you a Christian?" Kay remembers asking this question in her heart.

"Just as if he were reading my mind, Billy Graham, the man who was speaking that day through the television screen to my heart, started talking about our need to turn our lives over to Jesus Christ, who would help us be the kind of person we wanted to be. It sounded great, but I didn't know what it meant to 'give my life to Christ.' It sounded sort of scary. Nevertheless, after dinner I went to my room and prayed. Dr. Graham seemed like a man I could trust. So I told God I'd give my life to him for a year, to see what would happen."

Kay found a Bible and began reading a few chapters every night. As Kay continued to study the Word, she began to notice changes in herself.

"I was less concerned with rules and being 'perfect' and more concerned with pleasing God. Most of all, I had a sense of peace, a calm, and a confidence that remained in my heart despite what was going on around me."

The warm fellowship Kay experienced in the black church ignited within her a desire to attend a historically black college.

"It was important for me to go to a college where I was not a minority, somewhere where people understood me, my background, my hair. I wanted to have the freedom to join the pep squad, the sororities, or the math club if I wanted to, a privilege that was never really an option in junior or senior high."

Kay chose Hampton University, where the black power, black pride, and black-is-beautiful movements were in full blossom. She joined the InterVarsity Christian Fellowship (IVCF) on campus and couldn't get enough of the Bible studies and prayer meetings.

"My growing knowledge of the Bible led me to a greater understanding of who I am in God's eyes. One of my favorite passages during this period was Psalm 139:13–14, 'For you created my inmost being; you knit me together in my mother's womb. I praise you because I am fearfully and wonderfully made; your works are wonderful, I know that full well.'

"'I am fearfully and wonderfully made!' I would rehearse time and time again in my mind. It dawned on me that not only had God created me, but he had created me black. A newfound assurance in being black sprouted within me. I knew that God had created me in his image and that God didn't create mistakes. I realized that he knew what he was doing when he gave me kinky hair, a broad nose, full lips, and darker skin. These were beautiful physical features, not traits to be camouflaged in an effort to appear more white."

Kay learned how to share her faith and became more and more focused on her personal life in Christ. Hampton students were predominately from the Bible Belt, which made it harder to share the gospel.

"It is difficult for someone who has been brought up knowing only *about* God to become interested in *knowing* God. Further, the rise in power and prominence of Black Muslims also made it difficult. Malcolm X and his followers had labeled Christianity 'the white man's religion.' Those who followed Christ were looked down upon as having sold out to the white establishment. The militants argued that since white America had made itself rich on our backs, it owed us something. Seeing that the 'white devils' would never give us anything willingly, we were going to have to take it—by any means necessary."

Kay did not agree with their solution to the prejudicial turmoil that swirled around in our nation, but she could understand why their message had vast appeal for those who felt alienated in America. Their beliefs were built on hate, bitterness, and fear.

"I heard Jesus calling for us to forgive and move toward racial reconciliation. To the black militants, *love* and *forgiveness* seemed a show of cowardly weakness. In my mind, if black Americans worked to establish justice for all, it would be the most awesome display of power and love ever witnessed in America."

Kay graduated from college and learned about a job opening at the telephone company. She learned about the value of her education and her worth from the first interview.

"I must have interviewed well because they were puzzled as to why I was applying for an operator's slot. I mumbled, 'I thought that's all I was qualified to do around here.' The interviewer suggested that I was qualified for a management position, and would I be interested? Within a week I was hired as a manager at C&P Telephone Company."

For the first time in her adult life, Kay felt empowered, encouraged, and exhilarated. The telephone company treated her differently than she had remembered blacks being treated when she was a child. She remembered the teachers with Ph.D.s that taught at her school because that was the only place they could get a job. But it was different now.

"My coworkers didn't seem too shocked to be working with, and sometimes under, a black female. There were few instances where my race or gender even cropped up as an issue."

Corporate America began to realize that there was an untapped pool of talent out there, and Kay was on the upswing of that realization. A few thousand lawsuits helped with this process, and many firms were trying to protect themselves by aggressively trying to hire minorities.

Kay was promoted and offered a transfer to Roanoke, Virginia, shortly after being hired. Her college roommate was from Roanoke, and she introduced Kay to her future husband her first day there.

"I met Charles that night. He disliked me immediately, and I felt the same way about him. I classified him as a 'Roanoke hick,' and he thought I was a 'Richmond snob.' The problem was, that even before we met, Charles had promised my previous roommate that he would take me to dinner the following day for my birthday. He was a man of his word and kept his promise. So there we were the next night, gritting our teeth through what began as an extremely uncomfortable date. Through the uneasiness, God gave me a peace about Charles. I noticed that Charles was the brightest, most articulate man I had ever met."

Kay and Charles fell in love and were married within a year.

"One of the first things we did once we settled in was to try to find a church we both liked. We tried many black churches and loved the music and fellowship. But both of us had a strong hunger for more biblical teaching and less entertainment," Kay remembers.

"So on a lark, we dropped by a white church that one of our IVCF friends from college had recommended, Grace Church. It had everything we were looking for, except black folks. And that was a major obstacle. It was 1974, and 11:00 a.m. Sunday was still the most segregated hour in America."

Their first visit provoked many stares and whispers, but the pastor greeted them warmly at the door and made a special effort to introduce them to a few members of the congregation who, after an initial bout of shock, welcomed them.

"It became clear that the church was willing to try integration if we were. The question was, were we? After much prayer and hand-wringing, we chose spiritual growth over comfort and joined the church."

It didn't take long for church leaders to recognize Charles's biblical knowledge and solid faith, so they elected him as a deacon. While times were changing, there was still resistance in various places—even the body of Christ.

"I became involved in a weekly women's Bible study. One of the highlights of the year was a family trip to Myrtle Beach. All year long I heard people discussing the annual family beach trip. I had heard so many stories about the fun times they had together that I was really looking forward to going. But we were never invited. As summer drew near, I overheard women making arrangements for shared beach houses, but the conversation would die down whenever I came near. The group left for the beach without us, and I was crushed. I'd never felt so betrayed and rejected.

"Eventually my pain subsided enough for me to ask why we had not been included in the church vacation at the beach. An uncomfortable silence fell upon the room. 'Well, Kay, we just felt that—well, you know, there aren't many black people at Myrtle Beach,' one of the women said. 'We thought you would be uncomfortable.' I was so angry that it took everything I had not to lash out. Instead, I read a Scripture verse out loud before the group then said, 'I guess I thought that if we wouldn't be accepted at a certain vacation spot, that you would choose another one rather than leave us out.' Nothing more was ever said about it, but it was a hard-learned lesson for all of us."

Kay's career continued full steam ahead. She became a force manager for long distance and enjoyed her growing responsibility, but as she and Charles grew as a couple, they decided to have children.

"We had already made the decision that when we had children, one of us would stay at home with them. Charles was not the nurturer, nor did he have the ability to nurse a child, so we made the decision that I would stay home."

In June 1974, Charles Everett James Jr. was born, followed by about nine months of continual crying. Charles Jr. was a colicky child, clutching and clinging to his mother almost around the clock. A dark cloud hovered over the new family. The baby never slept more than a couple of hours a night. Eventually a compassion squad from the church came to help, and a few women would take turns spending the night with the Jameses so that they could get some sleep.

And then, rather unexpectedly, Kay found herself expecting another child, a girl this time.

"The timing of my becoming pregnant with Elizabeth was not good. Physically I was weak, and emotionally I was a wreck. Still,

I learned a valuable lesson from that experience that would later lead to an unknown horizon: *an unwanted pregnancy is not an unwanted child.* Even now, looking back, I can honestly say that all three of my pregnancies have been mistimed and unplanned, and yet all three of my children have been cherished additions to the family.

"I also learned, through my own experience, that women in unplanned pregnancies need the help and support of their family and community. Encouragement could be as simple as someone from the church coming over and having an adult conversation with me, or watching the baby one morning a week so I could run errands, or passing along baby clothes."

As the children grew older, Kay learned how she could reach out to other women who had unplanned pregnancies. Through a crisis pregnancy center called Birthright, Kay found the opportunity to minister to a number of black women who had the desire to have older, more experienced black women counsel them.

"I was horrified at what I learned and saw at the crisis center. I knew instinctively that killing an unborn baby was wrong, but I had never studied it as an issue. When I began to read the literature and see the pictures and became more educated about abortion, I felt very deeply about it."

Kay continued to volunteer at the crisis pregnancy center until her husband was promoted, and they were transferred to Richmond, where Kay had been raised.

Her mother moved in with them and helped Kay by cleaning house and taking care of the kids, giving Kay more free time. Determined not to let that free time got sponged up by the television, Kay set out on her first project, to restore her family by finding her dad and getting him help for his alcoholism.

Kay was persistent, and through prayer and diligence she tracked him down.

"I had checked into all the drug and alcohol treatment centers available. There wasn't much, and what was available was incredibly expensive. But I continued. For about six months I went through a cycle of driving around at night, poking through alleys and parks, looking for my dad. It didn't take long for my heart to grow sick. A string of lies and broken promises followed. It was traumatizing for me to see my father in such a low state, so I backed off entirely. My father's alcoholism eventually killed him."

When Kay realized that there was little more she could do for her father, she began to look around for part-time volunteer work. She was also looking for something that would empower the black community. She and Charles became testers with a fair-housing project. They would go in and try to buy or rent property to see if they were being discriminated against as blacks. It was a heart-wrenching confirmation time and time again that prejudice against blacks still thrived in America.

Kay and Charles began attending a new church, a sister Presbyterian church in Richmond. Once again they were the first black family in the congregation, but they couldn't walk away from the teaching, fellowship, and evangelism they found there.

"At Stoneypoint we met several folks fired up about the issue of abortion. A small group began praying about what sort of help we could provide. We decided to set up a crisis pregnancy center to reach out to pregnant women in need of assistance.

"I often talked with young women at the center who felt they had no other choice aside from abortion. Sometimes the baby's father had left, offering no support. Many girls were afraid to tell their parents. Other times a single parent with one or two children saw no hope of being able to manage yet another child. Yet I discovered that if someone sat down with each woman individually and provided her with some alternatives so that she had an option other than abortion, the overwhelming majority chose life."

During this time Kay was forced to come to terms with her relationship with her aunt and uncle. J. B. died unexpectedly, and her aunt died three years later.

"They say that the same sun that melts the butter hardens the clay. During my childhood, certain things had been as constant as the rain and setting of the sun. My father's neglect, my aunt's alcoholism, the heat of poverty and racism, and the emotional abuse from my aunt could have made me soft and needy, or bitter and hard. I melted. I realized that I spent all of my life trying to prove to my aunt that I wasn't the loose, no-good, nasty girl she thought I was. And I still catch myself trying to do that as I try to please and win approval. I spent most of my adult life trying to learn what made me react with softening rather than hardening. I have no other answer aside from the grace of God."

Kay had been working outside the home during this time at Circuit City in Richmond. One afternoon as she went in to resign, she was given a promotion and assigned to the regional headquarters in Beltsville, Maryland. After discussing it with Charles, they decided to accept the position. They knew that the cost of living was higher and that Kay would have to work outside the home.

About that time someone from the National Right to Life Committee called Kay to tell her that a black cable-television program was interested in doing a talk show on the abortion issue. They wanted her to represent the pro-life position.

"I laughed and said, 'Thank you, but no way. Nope. But thanks for calling,' and quickly hung up. However, when I told Charles and the kids about the unusual phone call, Chuck looked disappointed. He said, 'Kay, why don't you want to help save all those unborn babies?' Charles suggested that I call them back the next day, and I did, hoping that they had found someone else, but they hadn't."

Kay took the one-day job, still planning to work at Circuit City as planned. The debate was shown live during prime time.

"To say I was scared to death is an understatement. I hadn't slept the night before, and I hadn't eaten all day. All I could think about as they hooked me up to the wireless mike was how awful it would be if I threw up in front of all those cameras and they caught the sound on my mike."

Soon after the show aired, the executive director of the National Right to Life Committee called her and offered her a job. Kay resisted the opportunity.

"I looked forward to falling back into anonymity in my role as mother and manager. But the Lord had other plans. I became convicted in my heart that while this battle for the lives of millions of unborn children was going on all round me, I couldn't hide myself behind a good job selling stereos and TV sets."

That began a whirlwind three years of debating, giving speeches, holding press conferences, and traveling at home and abroad almost nonstop for Kay. She was both exhausted and exhilarated at the progress the National Right to Life Committee was making.

"I knew God had worked through me successfully when Faye Wattleton, the formidable spokesperson for Planned Parenthood, refused to debate me. During this time I learned to trust God for wisdom and even for the words I would speak. Two hours before we were to go on stage, I would lock myself in my hotel room with the phone off the hook and 'eat rug,'" Kay says, smiling. "'Eat rug' means to pray in the most humbling position possible, lying prone with your face down on the floor. From that vantage point I would confess to God my inadequacies and my fears. And I would ask him to speak his words through me."

God honored Kay's work, and while success loomed and strides were being made, at the request of her third child, Robbie, who was six at the time, Kay returned home to be a stay-at-home mom.

"I decided that if I saved every unborn child in America and lost my own, I would have failed in my life's primary mission. I thought about working part-time. And then came the heart-wrenching news that my mother was dying of cancer. I resigned from the National Right to Life Committee."

Temporarily, the family moved back to Richmond so that Kay's mother's last few months were the best they could give her. On her way out of town, Kay stopped in at the Bush campaign office to put in her opinion on a few issues close to her heart. When George W. Bush heard that she was there, he stopped in to see her.

"We had gotten to know each other when I was campaigning for pro-life candidates, his father included, throughout the past year. 'Kay,' he asked, 'Would you consider coming on board?' I flashed him my come-on-now, be-serious look. 'Really, Kay,' he continued. 'You're a natural. Would you at least consider it?' I said no, explaining that my mother had been diagnosed with cancer and the prognosis was not good. But it tickled me to have been asked.

"In her hospital room later on that day, I tried to encourage my mother before she went in for surgery. 'You know, Mama,' I said, 'I had an interesting offer today. George Bush Jr. asked me to come in and serve in the new administration! Can you imagine that? Of course I said no, but it just tickled me that he would ask.' Mama wasn't smiling. Lying prone on her hospital gurney, minutes before she went in for surgery, she proceeded to bless me out as only a black woman can do."

Kay called campaign headquarters at her mother's request from her hospital room. After they wheeled her mother out, she told George that based on skills and abilities, she wanted to join the administration in the highest position available stating, "I don't have a lot of time to make my mother proud."

Within a couple of days, Kay was asked to head up the public affairs team as the assistant secretary at the nation's largest agency, the U.S. Department of Health and Human Services. This sub-cabinet position had enough responsibility to require Senate confirmation. Kay was looking forward to her mother's being able to witness her swearing-in ceremony, but the confirmation process took so long that she was too weak to make the trip. She died four months later.

Kay continued to serve as a cabinet officer, but the pace was overwhelming at times and took its toll on her family. When an old friend called about a position with a nonprofit group dedicated to helping troubled youth, Kay jumped at the opportunity. Then after only a year away, Kay jumped back into the world of politics as a leader in the president's fight against drug abuse. Her insight on drug treatment, enforcement, and prevention came through first-hand experience with her father.

Kay went on to serve as the Secretary of Health and Human Resources for the Commonwealth of Virginia. One of the most challenging aspects of her job is deciding how to help people in need of food, money, and health care, without causing them to become dependent on the government for these things. Her opponents often accuse her of forgetting where she came from.

"I haven't forgotten," says Kay. "I remember the important role of hard work, self-discipline, and taking personal responsibility in my success and the success of other blacks whose lives began in poverty. I also haven't forgotten the racial slurs, the spit in my face, or the pinpricks I faced when I integrated into the schools. I haven't forgotten being turned away from housing simply because I'm black. And I most certainly haven't forgotten my childhood and the pain of going to bed hungry and cold.

"But as I look back over my life, I realize that God raised me up to be a leader by giving me a life full of learning. He began with a few lessons in humility in the slums of Portsmouth, Virginia, and then in Richmond, Virginia. But the chill of poverty and alcoholism was warmed away by the love of family and neighbors who brought healing to a broken home. He blessed me with an extended family of kin and community who taught me right from wrong and brothers who taught me pride in earning my way in this world.

"Black educators imbued an expectation of excellence. In breaking the color barriers as a schoolgirl, I learned the evil of racial hatred. In college God taught me to appreciate my heritage, to see that I am beautifully and wonderfully made. I graduated from college with the knowledge that I am his beloved child; it was the most important thing I learned in school.

"Finally, God gave me a husband whose sense of humor through all life's trials taught me resilient joy. My children have taught me the sanctity of life. And God gave me the opportunity to use my gifts and talents to speak for those who cannot speak for themselves:

unborn children. Most of all, there was Mama, the black sheep of the family, who taught me through her life the essence of love, the importance of family, and the meaning of faith. So, yes, God has been faithful to that little nappy black girl from the projects and fulfilled his Word in Jeremiah 29:11, 'For I know the plans I have for you,' declares the LORD, 'plans to prosper you and not to harm you, plans to give you hope and a future.'"

When a Child Dies

Featuring Joyce Wright

"Is something seriously wrong with my baby?"

Joyce Wright

BY ALL ACCOUNTS my pregnancy with my son, Matthew, was normal. Even when he was born, there didn't appear to be any obvious signs that an underlying problem existed. He was easygoing, healthy, and normal. But when Matthew was about five months old, I began to get concerned. I began to notice a lack of responsiveness from Matthew. He seemed excessively sleepy even for a newborn, and his muscle tone was poor. His eyes didn't follow his father and me as our firstborn's, Matthew's sister Sheryl's, did at the same age. And when I looked for his first smile, it wasn't there.

Initially, my husband Norm and I weren't too concerned, reasoning that he was just a little slower and that he'd catch up developmentally as time went by. But as I continued to watch my son, as mothers do, my nagging doubts built up, and my fears soon overwhelmed me. I realized something was seriously wrong. I responded the only way I knew how; I fell to my knees and told the Lord my fears. I asked him, before I even consulted professionals, "Is something seriously wrong with my baby?"

I knew instinctively that he was the only one who could give me the reassurance, comfort, and strength I needed and would have to have in the unknown years ahead. I longed for reassurance and knew I would not be satisfied receiving it from anyone but him. He had created Matthew, knitted him together in my womb, and blessed our lives with him. God could understand my fear, and although we didn't know what was wrong with Matthew, he did, so I knew he was the one I needed to go to for answers.

Although the Lord gave me peace as I prayed, he also revealed that the problem with Matthew was real. My mind in turmoil, I confessed to God that aside from his strength and guidance each hour of every day, I could not raise Matthew. And thus began the privilege of walking down a path as Matthew's mother for the following twenty-two years.

It wasn't too long after that initial prayer to God that Norm and I were away at a conference. We had left Matthew with my mother. While we were gone, he had some kind of seizure and stiffened in her arms. Then again, when Matthew was nine months old, he had his first grand mal seizure. His entire body stiffened, his arms and legs jerked uncontrollably, and his eyes rolled back in his head. I was terrified. We were outside with a neighbor, and I felt helpless as to what to do. With my eyes wide open, I cried out to Jesus while cradling Matthew in my arms.

Norm had been away at Green Oaks Boys Camp training counselors. When he rushed home in response to my emergency call, I blurted out, "Why weren't you with me? Why weren't you here when we needed you?" He looked so puzzled and vulnerable at my attack. I knew how unreasonable my questions were even as I asked, but when you feel so helpless, it's easy to be angry and lash out. Besides, Matthew's seizure had only lasted a few minutes, and he was OK by the time Norm arrived.

As I prayed about the situation, I experienced many emotional ups and downs. Overall, however, I knew in my soul that I hadn't been alone, that the Lord was there with Matthew and me as I called on his name. And I could rely on him even while living in this intense time of uncertainty. The bottom line was that he was my lifeline, the only one who was there all the time without fail.

Norm had a growing ministry, and there were going to be times when he was not around. The Lord was building character, strength, and faith in me as he, Matthew, and I weathered each of the following episodes.

As Matthew's seizures continued, we placed him under the care of neurologists at the UCLA Medical Center. After extensive testing the doctor confirmed our fears. During the development of Matthew's brain, something abnormal happened that caused severe retardation. And then, according to the doctors, at birth further brain damage occurred, which somehow caused seizures. The physician's final words penetrated our hearts. "Matthew may develop into a two-year-old mentally someday, and then again he may not."

When a parent is told such news, you grieve from the very marrow of your bones. All your expectations for that child are shattered. Matthew would never grow and develop like a normal child, attend college, marry, or have children of his own. He would never be able to express himself freely and share his likes or dislikes. For the remainder of his life, we were told, at best he'd have the mindset of a two-year-old. Even though we weren't surprised, we were thunderstruck. Our precious boy was so sweet, so wonderful in so many ways, and yet our hopes and dreams for him now lay in ruins. Norm and I prayed of course, but we also cried. We wept for what could have been.

Matthew's diagnosis changed our lives drastically. In the months and years ahead, multiple adjustments had to be made. First, we were constantly on the lookout for seizures. Because of this, we were less likely to have babysitting available to us, and we had to be highly selective in choosing sitters on occasions that required help. Because of his disability, when Matthew reached preschool age, he couldn't attend regular classes. And even then he was ill so much of the time and often so drowsy that he didn't benefit much from his special classes. We also were continually having to explain to others why Matthew didn't respond like other children. And over the years we had to go through the process of obtaining state funding for his training and then speak up for him every time the state decided to cut back on funds for the developmentally disabled. Additionally, our church had no facilities for a child like Matthew, so he had to be carried around for years. Consequently, whenever we took him anywhere, we had to carry a lot of extra equipment.

As the years went by, the daily grind really got to me. For all the reasons mentioned above, I was exhausted, discouraged, and isolated at home much of the time. I had little energy left to go out socially or even relax. I wondered if my endless list of chores was really important. My focus was on the daily care of Matthew, his older sister Sheryl, and Norm, and not much else.

Sometimes when I was discouraged, the Lord ministered to me. As I listened to old hymns, their familiar words ministered to my heart and built up my faith. As I listened to the words the music carried to my soul, I could let the tears flow. Looking back, I now see how important those times of tears were. I always tried to keep my composure for the sake of the rest of the family. So I would sing along, taking each phrase to heart. In return, my day would lighten a great deal. It also helped to look back and remember God's faithfulness and the significant things he had brought us through since Matthew's birth. He had experienced many illnesses and frequent high temperatures and seizures, but God always answered our prayers and carried us through those times.

It became clear as Matthew grew that he had a special ministry, one that he would not have had without his limitations. His calling was to teach and refine those around him, and that he did, even though he wasn't aware of it because of his lack of understanding. Norm and I developed a new sense of appreciation for each small sign of progress in Matthew's life. It took Matthew more than two years to reach out to grasp an object. Instead of taking that for granted as we had with our daughter Sheryl, we praised God for it. Additionally, we prayed for more than three years for Matthew to walk, and I was blessed to witness some tottering steps at the developmental school he attended. Then one evening all of us were sitting in the living room, and Matthew stood up, took four steps, and plopped down. Norm and I made some profound remark like "Isn't that great?" But our ten-year-old daughter said, "Why don't we stop right now and thank God for answering this prayer?" So we did.

In many ways we continued with life. Our vacation time was important, so in the summer we would load our car with porta-crib, stroller, playpen, and everything else and head for Montana to visit Norm's brother's family or go to Grand Teton National Park in Wyoming to fish. The vacations were a mixture of enjoyment, confinement, and hard work, but they were significant for all of us. Sheryl said those were her most enjoyable times with Matthew. A few years later Norm realized those trips weren't always a vacation for me, and we made some changes. The Lord provided a retired Christian nurse who could stay with Matthew for extended periods of time while we went north. What a difference it made to have a real break from the daily responsibility!

At times I experienced an overwhelming exhaustion. Some nights Matthew sat up and jabbered and squealed, and I didn't get much sleep. And over the years as we worked with various medications to control his seizures, it was a battle to maintain a balance and not under- or overmedicate him. Often we had to deal with various side effects as well. The doctors told me I probably would know better than anyone the level of medication that would be best for Matthew, so it was up to me to experiment and determine that level. This sometimes seemed to be an overwhelming responsibility.

But God was faithful and provided three essential people to walk beside me and give me input and strength. The primary person was my husband. Norm was committed to loving and raising our disabled child. I was assured early on that I could count on him. He was a zealous provider, juggling many jobs, sometimes working too much, and yet he was there to encourage me when I had doubts or needed a more objective view. The Lord had entrusted me with an awesome responsibility as Matthew's mother, and Norm was supportive and let me lead in his care. Norm was very much the head of our home in all areas, especially with our bubbly Sheryl.

The second person who was so important to me was my mother. She has been a wonderful example of trusting God each day, standing on Scripture during her own son's bout with cancer and early death. I was a young wife, spiritually immature, and had no experience with deep trouble. So watching my mother made a great impression on me. I saw God transform my brother's rebellious life, and I learned to look past the circumstances of illness and death to spiritual victory. My mother's example of faithfulness to God during her own difficulties was powerful. I knew her way was the only way I could get through my own tremendous challenge.

The third person God brought into my life was my best friend, Fran. Norm has a lot of friends, but I've had a tendency to be shy and a bit of a loner. Being married to an outgoing husband and minister and being home most of the time with a disabled child didn't help me to grow in that area. Fran had been my best friend since college. In Matthew's early years, she would call me saying that the Lord put me on her heart. Even though she had no disabled children, she was incredibly sensitive to what I was going through, and she would let me bare my soul. I can share anything with her, and she will listen sensitively and say, "Now we need to pray."

By the time Matthew was eight, my life seemed to be in constant crisis. He had frequent infections and high fevers that kept him out of his specialized school for weeks, and Norm worked long hours and continued to travel in his ministry. All that kept me off balance. Either Matthew was sick and needed a tepid bath in the middle of the night, or Norm was leaving for a seminar. In my most honest moments of self-talk, I wondered how much longer I could keep going. I was growing numb to life around me, with little interest or enthusiasm. Both Norm and Sheryl noticed the frustration in my voice and became concerned.

One day I met a friend at the local drugstore. I was there to get antibiotics for Matthew's latest infection. She had placed her son in a home for the disabled. I could see what a positive step it was for her. I was genuinely happy for her, but I was sure I would never do that with Matthew. I thought her circumstances were a lot different. Her son was hyper, so her house was frantic all the time. My little guy was sweet and easygoing, and I would never do it. But the next time I ran into her, I was again getting antibiotics, and I was exhausted. I had been up long hours with Matthew, fighting high temperatures. I wondered if there was a solution for us.

During this time Norm and I began to ask, "What's best for Matthew? What's best for us? Could someone else help him develop more than we can? Could someone else help him to lie down and sleep more at night, eat better, and learn some everyday skills? Could that someone give him better constant care than we can?" This process of questioning and searching occurred over a period of three years as we prayed, looked, and waited. We began to consider the possibility of a small, Christian residential facility for Matthew. We would not place him in a state institution. Eventually we discovered Salem Christian Home, which is run by the Christian Reformed denomination in Ontario, California. We took Matthew for an evaluation, and the staff said he would be a good fit in their multidisability ward. They would put him on the waiting list, and we could expect to wait from one to five years.

While we waited, I felt defeated in Matthew's care. He didn't eat well. I couldn't get him to lie down and sleep. He would sit up and giggle all night, leaving Norm and me exhausted the next day. We felt totally helpless to change the situation. I began to call the home, desperate for practical advice, and I soon realized the staff had knowledge that was workable. I saw they could give him better care than just one mom could manage.

A year later we received a call saying the home was ready for Matthew. All of a sudden, the time had come. We talked about how the change would affect us. There were so many positives to look forward to, but we had concerns as well. "What if our identity was largely based on caring for a disabled, dependent child? If he is no longer a part of our daily lives, how will we feel about ourselves?" Many parents, especially mothers, struggle with these issues when their children leave home. We also wondered if Matthew would forget us. Because of his limited mental ability, that was a real possibility.

We began preparations for taking him, and then the first disappointment hit. He came down with pneumonia, and his leaving was delayed. Weeks later he was well again, but the state funding had not yet come through, and the move was postponed again. Once the funding was approved and we had the go-ahead, Matthew became ill with mononucleosis.

Not only were we disappointed, but also now we began to question whether we had misread God's leading. Were we right or not? Then when Matthew was well, the home called and said we had to wait again since they were quarantined for two weeks. We really struggled with what was right to do. We felt as though we were on an emotional roller coaster.

Finally, everything was ready. We packed and took Matthew to the home, unpacked his things, and said good-bye. We wouldn't be able to see him for the adjustment period of six weeks. As we drove away, both Norm and I had such a sense of peace and calm that we began to feel guilty about it. What was wrong with us? We had just relinquished the care of our son to others for the rest of our lives, and we didn't feel upset or a sense of loss! And then it hit us. God in his wisdom had allowed us to go through those delays for several months, and we had worked out our feelings and adjustment in advance. And with the delays, instead of Matthew's being placed during the winter, at the height of the cold and flu season, the placement occurred during the summer, when he and the other residents had a greater chance of being well. There was a purpose. We saw that God not only prepared us for Matthew's arrival but also for the time when we would relinquish him to the care of others.

After Matthew's placement at Salem, I experienced an incredible lifting of my spirit because I was released from the physical demands of his care. I slept like never before, felt well, and looked around at my world with wonder and awe. I now had the opportunity for my personality to develop and blossom. For eleven years, it was as if I had taken a detour from life to carry a heavy but special responsibility, and I needed to reorient myself to life.

Before long we could see that Matthew was well, gaining weight, and in school more consistently. When he visited us at home, he seemed brighter and more alert. Life was obviously more meaningful for him.

He learned so much at Salem! He learned to walk up stairs, turn on a faucet, dog paddle in a pool, and feed himself. He didn't forget us, and he maintained his good-natured disposition. He seemed to enjoy music, and now and then he would sit at the piano and bang on the keys. Occasionally, he would throw his head back and laugh and clap his hands.

One of our most precious gifts from Matthew was his learning to hug. For fifteen years, we never received any response when we held him. We realize he was limited because his mental development never seemed to progress beyond an eighteen-month-old level. But something happened, and occasionally when we hugged him—perhaps two or three times a year—we would feel his arms around us, hugging us in return. And sometimes when we would look at him, open our arms, and say, "Matthew, hug," he would come to us with arms open in response. You can't imagine how we valued those responses.

In the spring of 1989, after Matthew had been at Salem about ten years, he went through a graduation program, complete with cap and gown, at the school he attended. He was twenty-one years old, and with his ambling gait and facial expression, he appeared even more physically disabled. His vocabulary consisted of only eight or ten words, and we never knew if he understood the meaning of even those few words.

We often took Matthew out to eat on our visits to Salem. One afternoon as we took Matthew back, he began to spit up his food. We had heard about the problem, but now we saw it for the first time. I talked to the staff about his regurgitation of some of his meal and then seeming to play with it. It was both a medical condition and a self-stimulating behavior. The problem continued, and we were able to observe it more. The Salem and school staff had tried many different ways to stop the repetitive behavior, but nothing seemed to work.

In the fall of 1989, Norm and I returned from conducting a marriage seminar, and when we saw Matthew, we were shocked. He had lost thirteen pounds, and he was already thin. Now he was down to ninety-one pounds. From that time on, the staff at Salem and the doctors treated the problem as a serious medical disorder—reflux esophagitis, a burning of the lining of the esophagus.

The specialist said there were medications to try but they didn't always work. And if they didn't, surgery might be necessary. Although the medical staff did all they could, the medication didn't work. The surgery would have to be done. An operation on the valve between the esophagus and the stomach that controlled the regurgitation response was required. Even with a fine medical staff, we realized we would have to depend only on our Lord.

The operation appeared to go all right, although the esophagus was thin as tissue paper from the effect of the stomach acids. It was torn during the surgery, but that was repaired. In the first few days after surgery, Matthew suffered complications, and infection set in. Daily I sat at Matthew's bedside and prayed on the phone with Fran. We were blessed to have been sustained by the prayers of Matthew's sister, his grandmothers, and our other friends as well.

One beautiful morning, as I drove to the hospital, this Scripture came on the radio: "For I am convinced that neither death, nor life, nor angels, nor principalities, nor things present, nor things to come, nor powers, nor height, nor depth, nor any other created thing, will be able to separate us from the love of God, which is in Christ Jesus our Lord" (Rom. 8:38–39 NASB). The phrase "death, nor life" seemed to stand out. I knew in my heart that Matthew's life was in the balance, and I marveled at the security we have in God's love.

As I visited each day, our time together was special. I patted Matthew's hand and talked to him in simple, loving words. He didn't reach out and respond, but his eyes followed me as I moved about the room. It was touching to see him content and peaceful, even during his times of discomfort.

After a week additional surgery was performed. Following the operation, Matthew stayed in the intensive care unit. He was heavily sedated and unconscious. There were eight tubes in him, and he was constantly on a ventilator. He developed adult respiratory disorder syndrome. We were hopeful when the fever dropped and his blood pressure stabilized, but in several days we could see that he was not responding. The doctors felt he was in the Lord's hands. We prayed at his bedside for the Lord's will to be done.

We stayed at our home the night of March 14 instead of at a motel near the hospital where Matthew was in ICU. I woke up at 4:00 a.m. with the feeling that Matthew was worse. I called the hospital, and the staff confirmed my fears. They had gone to full power on the ventilator. Around 7:00 that morning, as we were getting ready for the day, we received a phone call. It was one of the medical staff. He said, "We would like you to come to the hospital as soon as possible." His request didn't need any explanation.

Fortunately, we were able to speed through the traffic those sixty miles to the hospital. Both of us were aware that it could be Matthew's final hour. We had not seen any response from him for days.

When Norm and I walked into the room, the doctors told us that Matthew's lungs and heart were failing and would probably stop in about an hour. My initial response, which might surprise you if you've never had a loved one suffer and die, was profound joy. I was truly happy for him. I said, "Oh, he'll be in the presence of the Lord this day!" I knew he would be finished with the struggles of this world, totally healed, and finally out of pain. Both Norm and I felt that way. But we also felt helpless since there was nothing anyone could do to make Matthew well again. As much as we knew he was going to a far better place, we also knew we were facing the greatest loss of our lives.

We said good-bye to Matthew, and I prayed at his bedside, thanking the Lord for our precious child and for his provision of eternal life. As we stood there, we saw Matthew's pulse rate decline ten beats. We felt as though we were giving him back to God and saying, "He's yours. Have your perfect will with him." We believed God had something better for him.

Matthew's decreasing vital signs confirmed the reality that he was going to die soon. The doctors said we could stay there or wait in a family room. We chose the latter. Within an hour the doctors came to tell us Matthew had died. We cried and talked with them. God was truly loving and merciful when he took Matthew home that day, and we bowed to his perfect will. Perhaps others won't understand our mixture of feelings, but that's all right. We felt at peace.

I learned a lot about my husband from our son's death. It revealed to me his depth of emotion, love, and caring. I was amazed at how tender his feelings were and how easily the tears came for him. We were more aware of our oneness as we shared our grief and discussed how the Lord had gently prepared us for this time. Tears have also been a friend for me. Often they will come during a worship experience, and I become aware of the Holy Spirit's comfort and healing in my heart. They also come at some of the most unexpected moments.

The next few days were filled with arrangements for the funeral and people calling and coming by to express their concern. The morning of the service seemed to be going fairly well until our daughter, Sheryl, brought her own creative arrangement of flowers in a basket. She had also put in a small stuffed toy, along with our favorite picture of the two of them together. Seeing that triggered a torrent of tears that seemed to go on and on. But every time we cried, we realized we needed to and that we were using one of God's gifts.

Losing Matthew was a tremendous blow in and of itself. But like any major loss, it also caused a number of additional, or secondary, losses. The routine we had followed for years was gone forever. We would no longer look through catalogs to select his special sleepwear. We wouldn't have the special weekends when he would come home and stay overnight, nor would we be able to stop by Salem Home to take him out to eat. Instead, we would drive past where he used to live and keep traveling along the freeway.

We faced future losses as well. Matthew would no longer be at home on Thanksgiving or Christmas, nor would we take him to Knott's Berry Farm for his birthday. Those losses we could anticipate, but each week brought others we didn't expect. We couldn't call Salem anymore to see how he was doing; a topic of our conversation was gone, and certain phrases or expressions we would say to him would no longer be expressed.

Through Matthew's death, we learned in a new way about the grace of God. It came from the response of friends, people we knew, and others we hadn't even met. We learned about the value of their words, their silent presence, and their phone calls that continued not just for a few weeks but for years. We have seen how God has used Matthew's life to minister to others. It seems we now have a new ministry to parents who have lost a child in death. That's how God takes the upsets in our lives and gives them deeper significance.

Explaining the feeling of loss to someone who hasn't been there is difficult. There's nothing like it. Perhaps the word *devastation* describes it best. In the face of such loss, values change. Lifestyles are altered. Expectations once held so dear undergo radical surgery. The survivors wonder what will happen to them, how they'll make it.

When you suffer a serious loss, the well-meaning platitudes of others sound empty and insensitive and sometimes anger you. How do they know what will happen? Besides, you're numb. You're in shock. The loss wasn't expected. It's not what you wanted. How dare it invade your life and upset everything!

You keep returning to these questions: Why? Why me? Why us? Why now? In time, as the shock diminishes, you wonder how you'll survive because you're exhausted from continually riding an emotional roller coaster. Eventually, the questions turn to: What am I going to do? How will we make it through this? What do we have to do to survive?

When you receive the news of your loss, you are jerked from the safe, familiar routine of your life into the threatening and unfamiliar. The uncertainties will keep you off balance. After the shock subsides, your companions are fear, anger, anxiety, depression, denial, hysteria, and guilt. The roller coaster of emotions is enough to keep you questioning God's faithfulness.

But early in Matthew's life, before he had even been diagnosed, God had given me a passage that remained true throughout Matthew's entire life and even after God took Matthew home to be with him for all eternity. It is Isaiah 43:2–5: "When you pass through the waters, I will be with you; and through the rivers, they shall not overflow you. When you walk through the fire, you shall not be burned, nor shall the flame scorch you. For I am the LORD your God, the Holy One of Israel, your Savior. . . . Since you were precious in My sight, you have been honored, and I have loved you. . . . Fear not, for I am with you" (NKJV).

Surviving Life with a Preemie

Featuring Leslie Parrott

"I never felt God promising me a certain outcome about my pregnancy. The only thing I heard God saying was that no matter what happened, he'd be there for me, and that his grace was sufficient."

Leslie Parrott

A NORMAL PREGNANCY LASTS nine months, or about thirty-eight to forty-two weeks. Newborns are considered to be premature if they are born before they are thirty-seven weeks old. Statistics reveal that one in eight babies is born too soon. Although many risk factors can help to predict which pregnancies are at risk for premature delivery, in most cases no cause is found.

Among the risk factors that may increase the chances of having a premature baby are: having delivered a previous premature baby, which increases your likelihood by 20 to 40 percent; multiple gestation pregnancies such as twins; placental abruptions and placenta previa, which cause bleeding in the uterus; infections; diabetes; high blood pressure; fibroids; an abnormally shaped uterus; and cervical incompetence. Other factors include becoming pregnant while being treated for infertility, having a previous abortion in the second trimester, and the presence of certain birth defects.

In general, babies born after twenty-four to twenty-five weeks of gestation are mature enough to survive, although they will need a prolonged period of intensive care. Babies born at less than twenty-three weeks of gestation are usually not mature enough to survive. For even the smallest preemies, however, almost two-thirds of those that survive will either be normal or have only mild or moderate medical problems. For some women a premature birth can be a fatality.

For many women who give birth to a premature baby, the health risk for the child does not dissipate for years. Developmental and health problems often follow. This was the case of Les and Leslie Parrott, a couple who, after waiting over a decade to conceive, gave birth to a prematurely born child. This is Leslie's story of how she dealt with the pain and heartache, the letting go of expectations and grasping firmly to God's promises during her son Johnny's birth and the problematic years that followed.

"Most people think that because Les and I waited fourteen years after getting married to have a child, we struggled with infertility, but we purposely waited. We started dating when I was fourteen years old and Les was seventeen. We met in high school and casually dated, getting to know each other. We really enjoyed being together and didn't want to be apart, so I graduated a year early, started college a year after him, and worked hard to catch up academically so we could graduate together.

"After graduating from college, we got married and decided to go to Fuller Seminary together. At first I expected to move forward with having children, but we both felt called into ministry. So we made the deliberate choice to wait to have children so that we would both be equipped in the same manner educationally. After praying about it, I just felt strongly that if I had children, as much as I loved them, I would pour myself into them and wouldn't find any reason to write a dissertation. That took quite a bit of time because we were both earning our doctorates and trying to earn money at the same time. It felt like delayed gratification, but we were both committed to this plan.

"Then, once we finished, we just felt God saying, 'You know, you've given yourself to preparing. I really need you to focus on your ministry for while.' This was a real surprise and something I didn't want to hear. At different times Les and I would feel torn. Les would say, 'Let's start a family.' And I'd say, 'No, I feel really strongly this is not the time.' And then we would go back and forth. It was shocking to us that we wouldn't feel completely unified in that decision. It was a real test in our marriage, so we went to counseling to work through the stress. It still took a lot of negotiating and time before we both felt a yes in our spirits. It was a real difficult process, a lying-down, taking-up-your-cross kind of a issue for us. We both knew that God was not saying no to children; he was just saying, 'Not yet.' But it was hard because we're human; our desire for a family and our vision for our future included children.

"But the time came when we felt unity in our spirit that we were to work on a family, and we became pregnant right away. Because we have such a public ministry, we decided not to mention anything to anyone until we had gotten through the first trimester in case there was a miscarriage. I've always been a runner, so I continued to work out during my pregnancy. But shortly after the twelfth week of pregnancy, as I was running, I started hemorrhaging. The doctor referred me to a specialist and put me on bed rest immediately in order to try to save the pregnancy. From that moment on, I never got out of bed. Eventually I was hospitalized until Johnny was born.

"We were excited about having a baby but disappointed that we had waited so long to have a child only to be put on bed rest as soon as we got the good news. Nothing about the pregnancy was normal from that moment on, so we never got to celebrate with friends, and I wasn't able to say good-bye to the people I worked with at the university where both Les and I taught. Suddenly one day I was gone and never returned.

"I felt like maybe God was calling me toward a new role in my life, and he was preparing me for a separate monastic kind of time in my life that required total isolation. This was definitely not something I'd experienced previously. Les and I had a public marriage ministry, so this was going to be a change.

"Prior to the pregnancy, Les and I taught at the university every week and traveled, speaking together every weekend. We chose those specific opportunities so that we could be together as a couple. Then suddenly I was bedridden. Les is a man of his word, and we both felt impressed that he was to keep our teaching and speaking commitments, so there were eighteen weekends in a row where we were apart.

"It was an extremely difficult time for me because I was getting bad news on a daily basis about the baby and my health. Even more, I was worried. I never felt God promising me a certain outcome about my pregnancy. The only thing I heard God saying was that no matter what happened, he'd be there for me, and that his grace was sufficient.

"I really wanted the support of someone since Les was gone, specifically my mom. But she has severe diabetes, had gone through two heart attacks, and had a crippling nerve disorder that randomly flared up and caused intense pain. She was bedridden in another state, unable to travel. Since I'm an only child, she was, in essence, my family.

"Les and I decided not to decorate the nursery because the doctor said the percentages of our baby's survival at that point were very low. So we didn't want to fix it up and come home to an empty nursery. Additionally, I didn't have a baby shower or buy any maternity clothes because I was on bed rest. It was unlike any pregnancy I ever heard or dreamt of.

"The pregnancy was more than just the baby's life being threatened. I, too, was very ill. The specialist made clear that if there was a choice between the baby's life and mine, she would not intervene to save the baby. The only hope we had was if the baby made it to the twenty-eighth week of pregnancy, at which point we'd have to have a C-section. The problem with that option was that my health was so precarious the doctor didn't think I could live through a C-section. I had severe toxemia, and the best way the doctor could explain it was that my body was allergic to being pregnant. It was mind-boggling.

"Additionally, my internal system was not handling the pregnancy well at all. So we were in constant crisis mode, knowing that we were living a medical emergency and having to respond every day to the demands of survival for me while trying to nurture the baby. All that time I was trying to hold on to God's presence with no promise of an outcome. That was the hardest part.

"Looking back, I can see that God was working, but I was devastated. I felt useless and defective. I had a real sense of failure as a woman. Those thoughts seem irrational now, and of course I knew the truth theologically, but I felt like I was incapable of sustaining the life that was growing inside of me. I was supposed to be a place of refuge for this little baby to develop, and I wasn't able to do it on my own. Also, I felt like I was a completely noncontributing member of my marriage since Les had to cover for both of us in the ministry.

"I am used to being active, and suddenly I had to lie there and let other people serve me. It was so humbling, and I felt so powerless, like there was absolutely nothing I could contribute to anyone's life, including my child's. I felt utterly dependent on God's grace for the sense of my life's having value and worth. It was a defining time for me to learn the lesson of profound significance. God was teaching me that it's totally unearned.

"I cried out to God to save my child. I felt freedom to ask for everything my heart desired, and I did so repeatedly. I cried buckets of tears. I wasn't angry, but I was broken. I felt humiliated. I felt dependent. I felt like an infant myself. I've never felt the need of God more in my life than during that time. I kept journals during that time, and they are full of grief and prayers.

"Aside from my emotions, physically I was going through painful procedures. The doctors were giving me tests and amnios and requiring steroid injections every single day. But God's grace really was sufficient during that time. As someone who tends to amplify pain, I found that I was relaxed, able to face it without fear. It was what the Bible talks about when it says, 'And the peace of God, which transcends all understanding, will guard your heart and your minds in Christ Jesus'" (Phil. 4:7).

"Additionally, Les was traveling so much that I had to face the prospect that he might not be there when the baby came. As I lay in my hospital room one morning, the doctor came in to test my body for the strength and ability to have the baby, and they said, 'I think you have about five hours before your body shuts down. This is it.' The miracle was that it was the first day of the twenty-eighth week, the first day of the week that the doctor required before she'd do a C-section.

"Then the doctor said, 'We're going to schedule your C-section in a couple of hours.' Les had flown all night returning from a trip, and I was able to call him at home and wake him up so he could come to the hospital. He was with me when Johnny was born.

"The doctor held my baby up so I could see him, but I was out of it because of the medications they had me on. I was thankful that Les was there and able to follow our new baby into the neonatal intensive care unit. I don't think either of us was prepared to see our son in the condition he was in. He was so small he looked like a little Cornish hen. He was so tiny that he literally fit in the palm of my hand. Les put his wedding band on his arm and it went up to his shoulder. He was just a little peanut of a thing, and they incubated him immediately. They covered his eyes and his head and put him on life support. It could have really taken my hope away, but the fact that he was born and living was such a miracle to me, I just clung to that.

"Days of struggle turned into weeks, then months followed in the neonatal intensive care unit—all with no guarantees whatsoever. It wasn't enough that Johnny was born; now he had to survive. The doctors sat Les and me down and showed us pictures of all the possible outcomes of having a premature baby, which was a horrifying experience. They said that he could be mentally challenged and have severe retardation or have severe developmental problems.

"We knew that we loved Johnny, and no matter what the outcome, God had created him and given him to us as a gift. We had an intense attachment and love for him, but we also were torn with the possibility that he would suffer. We could see the enormity of the task ahead of him, and in comparison to his size we thought it was horrendously out of balance.

"Johnny spent the first three and a half months in the neonatal intensive care unit, during which we did around-the-clock vigils. During the first two weeks he sustained his life, but he wasn't able to eat, and he wasn't gaining weight. In fact, every baby loses weight after birth, but when they weigh only one pound and eight ounces when they are born, and they drop below a pound, it's a life-threatening crisis.

"The doctors had me pump my breast milk because Johnny's immune system was virtually nonexistent. The nurses fed him through a small tube, giving him three drops of milk, and then he'd stop feeding. It was exhausting to have to pump milk knowing that your child isn't going to drink it and get the nourishment that God put in it. But I pumped my breasts around the clock, every two hours, so he would have fresh milk to nourish his immune system. I was willing to do whatever it took to help my son survive.

"He continued to lose weight and was rushed into emergency surgery. Initially the doctors didn't know what was wrong. They just knew that without intervention he was not going to make it. I watched them put this tiny one-pound baby on an eight-foot gurney, surrounded by technicians and life-support machines, and wheel him into surgery. As I watched the swinging doors close behind them, I was faced with the possibility that he might not ever come out again.

"The doctors performed the most remarkable surgery. It was a procedure that had been around for only a few months. It was a drastic procedure. They had to take everything out of Johnny's body because he was so small that they couldn't even get in there to operate. Once inside, they realized that Johnny had necrotizing enterocolitis, an inflammation of the intestines. As a result, he couldn't process his food, and an infection had started. The doctors fixed the problem and literally put everything back into him. Even now the procedure amazes me.

"But concern didn't stop there. Next Johnny had to survive the recovery process, which was the scariest time of all because he was already on life support, but now his body was just consumed with intense pain throughout his system.

"I remember watching the monitors and hanging on every noise they made. I could see how concerned the nurses were about his survival. I could feel the heaviness in their expressions. I had no idea what would happen. There was a beautiful Christian nurse who was John's primary caregiver at night, and she became so committed to our family. She prayed over him and encouraged me that God was in control.

"One night at midnight, as she prayed for Johnny, his monitors began to slow down, subsiding from the rapid beating that only reminded us that his life hung in the balance. It was like there was an instant moment of transition for him where he relaxed and began to start healing. Johnny had been prayed for a lot before that time, but God made a clear, profound moment of grace come to our attention during prayer. It was a spiritual breakthrough. From that point on he took a turn for the better, and I got to hold him for the first time. He was three and a half weeks old.

"Other crises followed. He had intraventricular hemorrhage, bleeding in the brain. He had retinal damage, and his lungs collapsed on different occasions. Every time something happened I knew that I could lose him.

"Once he was stabilized somewhat in these areas, the biggest concern was getting him to gain weight and grow. When he was two months old, he still hadn't reached two pounds. When he reached the two-pound mark, the nurses made a huge sign and put it on the wall! It said, 'John Parrott is two pounds today!' It was exciting for all of us.

"Johnny was able to come home when he finally reached the three-pound mark, but he remained on monitors and had to have an oxygen tank. He was three and a half months old at that time. Bringing him home was both exhilarating and terrifying. I thought, *I don't even know how to be a mom to a normal, healthy baby, much less a premature baby who is so sick.* I wanted to do things right so that he wouldn't get sick again. I felt terror that his life could be in my ability to care for him. My level of anxiety was abnormally high.

"Johnny had a lot of stomach problems due to an undeveloped reflux. This caused him to have projectile vomiting every time he ate. As a result, he literally screamed in pain for about twenty hours a day for the first year of his life. He didn't learn to smile until he was over seven months old. Developmentally he was delayed because every fiber of his body was going toward surviving. He just didn't have any brain energy left for developing.

"I was exhausted. I had never been so tired in my life. One afternoon a friend of mine came to visit, bringing with her one of those large exercise balls. She had read in an article that they had been successful at comforting colicky babies. The second I sat on it and starting bouncing up and down with Johnny, he stopped crying. From that point on, I literally sat, bouncing on that ball fifteen hours a day.

"There were other problems. The doctors said that Johnny could have cerebral palsy. And due to the fact that he came close to the highest level of retinal disease, there was a possibility that he would be blind. This meant that Johnny would have to have eye surgery. Again people banded together and prayed specifically for his sight and against cerebral palsy. God heard their cries and didn't allow John to be blind or to have cerebral palsy. Les and I were bewildered, mystified, and grateful beyond words.

"John continued to be ill, even after he was released from the hospital. After the surgery he got pneumonia. His lungs were very weak. We had to call 911 three times and have him transported by ambulance to the hospital because his breathing was so bad. We had moments like that until Johnny was four years old.

"Johnny has had to have a lot of occupational and speech therapy. He didn't say any words until after he was two years old. We waited and watched, having no idea how things were going to unfold for him. He was given neurological exams, and we were thrilled when they told us that he had no neurological deficits.

"Johnny continued to struggle with terrible reflux, throwing up everything he ate until he was almost five, causing a full food aversion. We have had to do a lot of interacting work with him to help him overcome it. It's a normal response for someone who has had such negative experiences with food. To him, eating isn't pleasurable; it's a place of pain and fear. Because of his reflux, he had never tasted meat, vegetables, or fruit until after he was five years old.

"Nothing about the life of a preemie unravels naturally or easily. On the other hand, we notice that Johnny is the most social, verbal, loving, playful, imaginative child. He connects well with people because he's had a crowd around him since birth.

"Johnny has asked me, 'Mommy, why are some babies born early like me?' He notices he's different in some ways, like the scar on his tummy from his first surgery. Les and I have taken advantage of those opportunities to explain to him what a gift and miracle he is from God, and that the scar is a sign of that gift. We just explain that the scar is our special mark, a reminder that God saved his life.

"This year Johnny is six years old and going half a day to kindergarten. The doctors say he will probably have no lifelong ramifications aside from a slightly weaker immune system and some minor underlying conditions. Doctors had told us that by the time he was five we would know if he was out of the woods. They also told us that a third of children born premature end up profoundly disabled, a third are mildly impacted, and a third have no effects whatsoever.

"A year after Johnny's fifth birthday, Les and I had another baby. It took a long time for me to have the courage to try it again. I really didn't know if I could go through that again if faced with a similar situation. In response to my fears, the doctors said that the conditions I had with Johnny were one in a million. Taking that in stride, I thought maybe I'd be able to experience a normal pregnancy. But that was not the case. As soon as I got pregnant, I had complications, and I was placed on bed rest and then hospitalized with the same thing I had before. I had five amnios before Jack was born. It became a lighthearted joke at the doctor's office where I had to go to have all the invasive testing. They said that by the end of my second pregnancy they should name a memorial suite after me.

"When Jack was born, they tested his lung maturity. For an infant to be born and breathe on his own, the results needed to read in the forties, his was twelve. So I thought, *Here we go again to the neonatal intensive care unit. He's going to be incubated.* He was taken to the neonatal intensive care unit for eight hours. During the ninth hour they said he was so healthy they took him off breath support and moved him into my room. And he has been a normal, healthy baby ever since.

"God was faithful and went with us through the crisis. But when you are going through difficulty, it's sometimes hard to see that. When you haven't slept through the night for over two years, and you haven't even had two consecutive hours of sleep for all that time, you're unable to function normally. There were days when I was so sick or tired that I couldn't even read my Bible. That's when God's faithfulness to me became so evident—during those times where it took everything I had to survive.

"Other people were helpful to us, but when the visible crisis had passed, they moved on with their lives. Those are probably the moments when I experienced God's grace in the most unexpected ways. I felt a lot of guilt about not spending time with the Lord. One really liberating thing for me during that time was taking away the spiritual to-do list.' Instead, I looked for other ways to worship God. One way was to have my friend come over and pray with me while I bounced Johnny on the exercise ball. It drove her nuts, but it was all I could do. God's grace abounds during times like these.

"When God doesn't promise you the outcome you desire but promises you that he'll be there, going through your crisis with you, it is easy to lose focus. God blessed us with healing in Johnny's life, and we realize that for many couples, that is not the case. We can't understand why, but what we do know from personal experience is that God answered our cries and was faithful to be with us as he promised, in the midst of the unknown, pain, heartache, and fragile moments of time when we feared death the most. His promise in Jeremiah 29:13 is true; 'You will seek me and find me when you seek me with all your heart.'"

Walking through Depression

Featuring Joni Eareckson-Tada

"Jackie, you've got to help me. They're keeping me alive. It's not right . . . you've got to help . . . give me something—you know—an overdose of pills.

Look, I'm already dying. I'm suffering. Can't you help me end the suffering? Please—cut my wrists—Please! Do something."

Joni Eareckson-Tada, *Joni*

ON JULY 30, 1967, the world stopped spinning for Joni Eareckson-Tada; judgment was at her doorstep, and death was only a breath away. While vacationing near the Chesapeake Bay, Joni dove into shallow water and broke her neck, leaving her body permanently disabled. In an instant the seventeen-year-old budding artist and horse enthusiast became a quadriplegic. To Joni life was over, but to God it had just begun. He had a plan for Joni's life, a plan for good and not for evil, a plan to give her hope and a future. He knew it wouldn't be easy for her, but he also knew Joni, and he knew she would be just the one to fulfill his will in the years to come. She would eventually call on him in her darkest days, and he would listen. When she turned to him with all her heart, he would be there.

"'I will be found by you,' declares the Lord, 'and will bring you back from captivity'" (Jer. 29:14).

Thirty-eight years later Joni has literally touched the lives of millions as a result of her obedience to God, by creating an international ministry called Joni and Friends. Joni has been more successful in sharing her love of the Lord without the use of her legs than most people have with full use of their body. If you asked her today whether it was all worth it, she'd enthusiastically say yes! But if you asked her during her first two years of recovery, she could not have envisioned the joy she now knows. Instead, she would have told you about the gallons of tears that fell to the floor in the hospital ICU unit, as well as her severe chronic depression, her frustrations and fears, her horror, shock, grief, remorse, and anger, not to mention her thoughts of suicide.

Joni is not the only person who has ever suffered from depression that led to thoughts of suicide. The National Institute of Mental Health reports that 18.8 million American adults suffer from clinical depression. Additionally, in 2001, suicide was the eleventh leading cause of death in the United States. Adverse life events in combination with depression can be a deadly mix when not tempered by the Healer of our souls.

This is the story of how Joni overcame those dark days and how, through Christ, she was able to stand up against depression and thoughts of suicide. Through her example, others can apply the same tools to their lives.

When Joni was first injured and lay in a hospital so many years ago, they put her on a gurney and wheeled her into a therapist's office. She had a lot of questions like, How am I going to make it? and How am I going to move beyond this depression? No one offered satisfying answers, and her future seemed to hang precariously in limbo.

During her entire first year of recovery, she was often placed on a Stryker frame—a long, flat canvas device that she had to lie on for a couple of hours. After awhile the hospital staff would strap a piece of canvas on top of her and flip her over so she was face down. While in this position, she kept a mouth stick in her teeth and laboriously turned the pages of her Bible, searching for answers. But the Bible seemed irritatingly out of touch with her current situation. She kept coming across phrases like "rejoice in suffering." Choking on these words, she grew even more frustrated, especially as she faced the harsh reality of never walking again.

"Oh, God, how can you do this to me?" she prayed through tears. "What have you done to me?" She was devastated. Grief, remorse, and depression swept over her like a shroud she couldn't remove. She didn't understand at that point that suffering cannot be explained or understood in a neat and tidy fashion. When we scream out our whys to God, we're asking with hot emotion why he allowed such a thing to happen. Joni's circumstances seemed unbearable, and as depression and frustration settled in, she began to entertain thoughts of suicide. She spent hours imagining different ways to do it. Pills would be easiest, but she feared the nurses would find her and pump her stomach. She asked her friend Jackie to slash her wrists, but she refused. She hoped that some kind of hospital accident would kill her.

One night as she was trying to get to sleep in her Stryker frame, she considered her attitude of bitterness and how she had allowed herself to become so despondent. She tried to pray and couldn't. She searched her memory for some promises from God's Word to encourage herself, but nothing proved reassuring. She was angry because of her helplessness. She silently wished for enough strength and control in her fingers to find a way to end her life. Tears of rage, fear, and frustration followed as she laid in a facedown position questioning God's sovereignty and existence.

"No one else is being punished like this. Why did God do this to me? How much more can I take? I'm at the end of my rope, and God doesn't care. Why, God, why? And for that matter, who or what is God? Certainly not a personal being who cares for individuals," she reasoned. "What's the use of believing when your prayers fall on deaf ears?"

When you're hurting, you feel like your heart is being torn apart. You're numb, and you don't know if your emotions are upside down or right side up. Joni had plenty of Bible verses to look at and many reasons to consider why she was in her current circumstance, but when you're in the midst of so much pain, Bible verses often sting like salt poured on a wound. Besides, a bleeding heart doesn't stop just because you find answers that may appear good, right, or true. Pat answers are great for SAT exams or pop quizzes, but they mean little when you're grieving.

In retrospect Joni now can clearly see that self-pity was consuming her. In fact, she was drowning in it and in return wanted to hurt God. To her the only way she knew to hurt him was to deny him along with the rest of the world. She became even moodier and disassociated from the outside world by taking fantasy trips. She'd sleep late in order to dream or take naps to escape or fantasize. By concentrating, she was able to shut out completely her present reality.

One day after she was released from the hospital, she was sitting in her wheelchair at her family's farm in Sykesville. Friends who had come to see her had saddled horses and gone off on a trail ride. She felt self-pity pour over her as she compared her situation to theirs. While warm summer sunlight glimmered through the nearby branches of large oak trees, creating bright patterns on the lush grass underneath, Joni closed her eyes and visualized a similar day two years earlier.

In her mind she was with an old boyfriend, riding horseback toward the forest, across the fragrant meadows, where they stopped in a deserted place and jumped off their horses. She relished memories of unrestrained pleasure, excitement, and sensual satisfaction—feelings she knew she had no right to enjoy then or relive now.

When the Holy Spirit convicted her, she rebelled even more. "What right have you to tell me I can't think of these things? You're the one who put me here! I have a right to think about them. I'll never enjoy sensual feelings and pleasures again, but you sure can't strip away my memories!" she argued.

The more she daydreamed about these experiences, the more withdrawn she became. She was frustrated and bitter and blamed God. In response, she emptied every physical pleasure from her mind and threw it up to him in bitterness. She refused to accept the fact—God's will, she presumed—that she'd never do or feel sexual pleasures again. So she rebelled.

Her fantasy trips became longer and more frequent. And when she ran out of memories that she thought would anger God, she created new ones. She developed wild, lustful, sexual fantasies that she was sure would displease him. She scoured her past because it momentarily allowed her to avoid the truth of her present circumstances.

"People often ask me," Joni stated recently, "when the change came. Where was the turning point? What was the milestone that freed you from your depression?"

One night during a desperate prayer, Joni realized she had two choices as she prayed: "God, either you exist or you don't. If you don't exist, then there is no logical reason for living. If people who believe in you are only going through the motions, I want to know. Why should we go on fooling ourselves? Life is absurd most of the time. And it seems man's only end is despair. What can I do, Lord? I want to believe, but I have nothing to hang on to. God, you've got to prove your existence to me!"

The Lord heard Joni's petition and answered her.

Weary from her prayer, she closed her eyes. Then from out of nowhere, an incredible calmness came over her. A still, small voice softly whispered, "Thou wilt keep him in perfect peace, whose mind is stayed on thee" (Isa. 26:3 KJV). She sensed God's presence and felt him reaching out to her. He reminded her from his Word, "My thoughts are not your thoughts" (Isa. 55:8).

Then she remembered the Bible verses she previously thought were irritatingly out of touch with reality. Things like, "Consider your afflictions light and momentary" (see 2 Cor. 4:17). And they became real to her. God promises to reward those who diligently seek him, and the more she searched for answers from the Bible, the more she understood. She forced herself back into God's Word. She refused to dwell in self-pity and drown in her tears. God was providing her with yet another test—a gut testing of his truth, love, and purposes.

In turn she needed to repent for pushing God away. "Lord," she cried out, "I've been wrong—wrong to try to shut you out. Forgive me, God. Please forgive me and bring me back to you, back into fellowship with you once more."

As she began to pray and depend on him, he did not disappoint her. She recognized how she had tried to manipulate her prayers to get what she wanted, saying, "Lord, I want to do your will, and your will is for me to get back on my feet or at least to reclaim the use of my hands." She was deciding God's will for her life, and when things didn't turn out as she planned, she rebelled.

Joni wept for all the lost months filled with bitterness and sinful attitudes, and she daringly prayed for God's will for her life, finally letting go of her own. In order to accept God's will for her future, she had to believe that everything that had happened to her, including the accident, was an important part of his plan. One day as she was reading the Bible, she came across these words: "In every thing give thanks: for this is the will of God in Christ Jesus concerning you" (1 Thess. 5:18 KJV). She wondered if it was really God's will for her to be thankful in everything and decided to blindly trust him on this one verse. She thanked God for what he had done in her life and for what he was going to do.

We aren't always responsible for the circumstances in which we find ourselves. Consider Joni's accident. If you had asked the young seventeen-year-old diving into Chesapeake Bay that hot summer day if she wanted to be a quadriplegic, she naturally would have said no. Now consider your own circumstance for a moment. Are you hurting? Do you feel rejected? Have you been forsaken by your husband, forgotten by your friends, lost a loved one to sickness or death? Are you struggling with infertility or the loss of your health? Do you feel the world has passed you by? Are you so angry with God that you refuse to accept his will over yours?

As women after God's own heart, we must remember that the most God-forsaken man who ever lived was Jesus. No matter what you are struggling with, Jesus confronted it on the cross. He agonized over your pain and suffering as he tackled the cross.

When we're suffering, we want answers. We want assurance that there is a reason for our pain that somehow transcends our problems. We want to be reassured that our world is not coming apart at the seams. We want a guarantee that our world is orderly and stable and somehow safe. We want assurance that our life has a purpose.

Joni had a crucial conversation with her dad during one of those early days after her accident. She had grown quiet and withdrawn, wrestling with depression.

"What's the matter, honey?" her dad asked.

"I don't know, Daddy. I'm just sad, depressed."

He nodded and in wisdom listened.

"I don't know if I can ever really adjust to being paralyzed," she told him. "Just when I think I've got things under control, I go into a tailspin."

Joni knew her parents would do anything to help her, but she felt defeated.

"I guess the thing that affects me most," she continued, "is that I'm so helpless. When I think about home, I remember the things you built and created. It's really sad to think that I can't leave a legacy like you. When you're gone, you will have left us with beautiful buildings, paintings, sculpture, art. I can never do any of that. I can never leave a legacy."

Her dad wrinkled his forehead for a moment, then bestowed profound wisdom to his daughter. "You've got it all wrong. These things I've done with my hands don't mean anything. It's more important that you build character. Leave something of yourself behind. You don't build character with your hands."

Her father was right. But in the midst of her depression, she didn't recognize this as truth. She silently wondered how she could leave something of herself behind if she was paralyzed from the neck down. It just didn't make sense. But when she looked through the Bible for answers, she learned that God would move her out of the "school of suffering," out of her current circumstances, in his own good time. The apostle Paul put it this way: "Don't stop striving." Even at the peak of his life and commitment to Christ, Paul admitted he had not arrived spiritually.

As Joni slowly began to mature in her faith in Christ, she developed a new understanding about suffering. Rather than trials to avoid, she eventually began to see suffering as an opportunity to grow in her faith because God gives so much of his love, grace, and goodness to those who are suffering.

Resting and trusting in God, Joni stopped asking why as she had so many times before. As she matured in Christ, she became more relaxed because she knew he was in control. It was not a blind, stubborn, stoic acceptance; she was becoming more and more intimate with him and realizing that he is worthy of her trust. She has realized that although she is fickle and plays games, God does not; and although she has been up and down, bitter and doubting, he is constant, ever loving. She reasoned that there were others in worse circumstances than she and reminded herself that the apostle James wrote of people who were being torn apart by lions. Certainly their lot was far worse than hers. And if God's Word was sufficient for their needs, she became confident that it could definitely meet hers.

Joni reminds us through example that regardless of what you may be enduring, pain and suffering serve a purpose. We don't always see this clearly, especially in the midst of a difficult circumstance. But the apostle Paul suffered extensively for Christ. His experience included imprisonment, beatings, stonings, shipwrecks, and a physical "thorn in the flesh" (2 Cor. 12:7 KJV). There is a blessing to suffering. One of Joni's favorite quotes is from J. B. Phillips, who said, interpreting Romans 5:3–5, "We can be full of joy here and now even in our trials and troubles. Taken in the right spirit, these very things will give us patient endurance; this in turn will develop a mature character, and a character of this sort produces a steadfast hope, a hope that will never disappoint us."

This change in Joni's attitude began after two years in the hospital. After two years of bitterness, anger, depression, and self-pity, Joni turned to Jesus to comfort her. Then there were nights when instead of being a stoic, she would visualize Jesus coming to visit her. She pictured him breaking the hospital rules and sneaking into her room, where he walked over to her bed and put the guardrail down and sat on the edge of her mattress. She would imagine him gently brushing back her hair with one hand while showing her his scar from being nailed on the cross on the other. Then he spoke to her tenderly saying, "Joni, if I loved you enough to die for you, then can't you trust me with the answers?"

God becomes what we need when we are hurting. In Psalm 18, he becomes the high fortress to the person like Joni who was scrambling for meaning, who's looking to be rescued. And in Psalm 2, he becomes the father to the orphaned. In Isaiah 54, he becomes the bridegroom to the widow. In Isaiah 62, he becomes a husband to the single woman who grieves over her unmarried state. And in Exodus 15, he becomes the healer to those who are sick. In Isaiah 9, he becomes a wonderful counselor to the mentally ill. In John 4, he is the living water to those who are thirsty, and in John 6, he is the gateway to heaven for those who look beyond this world.

How or why God created suffering is not the question. Instead, Joni advises wisely, we should focus on the fact that he's the answer and we need him.

"When I finally figured this out, I looked through the Bible with my mouth stick, and I suddenly realized that God is supremely good in the midst of suffering. Not because he gives answers but because he *is* the answer. He doesn't offer frivolous words absent from meaning; he is the Word and the meaning behind it.

"I guess that's why I love 2 Corinthians 4:7–10 so much. 'Though we are handicapped on all sides,' it says in the J. B. Phillips translation, 'we are not crushed. Though we are perplexed, we're not in despair. Though we are persecuted, we're not abandoned. Though we are knocked down, we are not knocked out.'"

Overcoming Sexual Abuse

Featuring Beth Moore

"By the time I was seven, I was terribly ashamed of myself. I always remember sitting in church with my head down. I wore my shame like a coat."

Beth Moore

A BEAUTIFUL TEENAGE PRINCESS named Tamar enjoyed all the benefits of her father, King David, and his kingdom. Her future undoubtedly held the best he had to offer: honor, wealth, respect, and the opportunity to marry a prince or king of equivalent stature. But her half brother Amnon, overcome by her beauty and his own lusts, irrevocably changed her joy and innocence. Pretending to be sick, he asked Tamar to bake him some goodies in order to make him feel better. When she brought the freshly baked sweets to him, he swept them aside and raped her. She protested, resisted, and begged him not to disgrace her, but he continued with his premeditated attack. This moment of willful indulgence ultimately resulted in a life of suffering for Tamar.

Tamar is only one of countless women sexually assaulted throughout history. Unfortunately, children are also victims of such abuse.

Recent studies from local child protective service agencies identified approximately 126,000 children as victims of either substantiated or purported sexual abuse per year; of these approximately 75 percent are girls. Nearly 30 percent of these victims are between the ages of four and seven.[1] To say that the effects of abuse are rampant in the world today is an understatement. And those who perpetrate sexual assaults target both Christians and non-Christians alike.

The English word *abuse* is translated from the Hebrew *alal,* which means, "to do harm, to defile." Sexual abuse against children occurs when inappropriate physical, visual, or verbal interactions are instigated by an adult against a child. Nothing interferes with a child's sense of esteem or destroys trust more completely than sexual abuse. Further, it steals their innocence and relentlessly haunts them throughout adulthood.

Many abuse victims believe that healing cannot occur until they erase every memory of the abuse, but this is not possible. Nor can the pain, fear, and shame associated with those memories vanish overnight. The road to recovery often requires a heavy time commitment.

Following is the story of Beth Moore, a self-proclaimed "army brat," raised at First Baptist Church in Arkadelphia, Arkansas, who gave her life to Jesus before she was six years old, shortly after a friend of her family began to abuse her sexually. But what the enemy intended for evil, God used for good, and he called this fragile, broken child out of obscurity and into the spotlight in order to lead others to the saving knowledge of Christ and the power of healing found in the Holy Spirit.

"My mother, Aletha Green, who passed away in 1998, once told me that in my earliest years I was strong willed and forthright about everything that was on my mind. But my natural tendency to speak out was suddenly stifled when I became a victim of sexual abuse before the age of five by someone close to my family. This experience had a devastating effect on my personality. The abuse was intermittent, but it continued until I was nearly out of elementary school. Once it began, I became terribly insecure. I withdrew from others and was often close to tears, pulling my hair out by the handfuls. And while there were wonderful things unfolding during my childhood, they were overshadowed by the victim mentality I had developed. During my critically important developmental years, the effects of abuse wove its way into the fiber of everything I did, including the relationships I formed.

"Like most childhood victims, I told no one about the abuse, not even my family. As I grew into my teens and early twenties, I fell into a cycle of defeatist thinking due to the habitual pattern of sin, remorse, and repentance that proved to be even more difficult to grapple with than the abuse itself.

"As a Christian, I assumed I needed to ignore the pain because I thought that was the object of the Christian life—to forget, cover with a mask of piety, and move on. But by the 1980s, when I reached my thirties, right after I'd written my first Bible study, God showed me that I had to deal with the pain I had kept hidden for so long. Like a nine-foot Goliath demanding my attention, I was forced to confront the anguish of those years long ago. The healing, however, did not come easily. It was an extremely rough season in which I absolutely despaired of life.

"But a miraculous thing happened as I dealt with the pain. During those long, dark days, God called on me to be a writer and minister of his Word. At the same time I know without a doubt that

Satan was trying to destroy me; he knows his biggest threat is somebody learning to wield the sword of the Spirit. He had tried to break my spirit and my love for God once before, through sexual abuse, and he knew that if I spent time in the Word and encouraged others to do the same, healing would occur. But his persistent attacks only made me more determined than ever to pursue God.

"I had been studying the Scriptures intensely for five years under the tutelage of Buddy Walters, who was teaching a Bible class at Houston's First Baptist Church. Buddy's passion for God's Word inspired me so much on that first day of class that as soon as it was over I ran to my car, shut the door, looked up toward heaven, and said, 'I have no idea what that was, but I want it!' The Lord's response, amazingly enough, was instantaneous. It was like he took a match and struck it across a stone, lighting in my heart a lifelong love affair with him.

"God's Word is not only health and life to my soul but also to the very marrow of my bones. God has made clear that his Word is alive and powerful. This supernatural encounter with my heavenly Father marked the beginning of my healing. But full deliverance didn't come until I learned, through Bible study, the significance of the Holy Spirit in my life. God not only exposed the victim in my heart and worked to heal my pain, but he also showed me how the Holy Spirit and the power of his Word could change my life. It made the difference between living a life of cyclical defeat and walking in victory.

"I prayed that my self-destructive flesh would be crucified and that the Spirit of the living God would be resurrected and live in me, and this made all the difference. I am grateful that God chose my healing to be progressive rather than immediate because I learned to depend on him every moment, and that's when I fell head over heels in love. Slowly, breath after breath, the Holy Spirit entered my lungs like desperately needed CPR; and it completely transformed me. The role of the Holy Spirit is absolutely crucial to the process of healing from sexual abuse because he inhabits us, dwells within us, and overtakes us, giving us the power to live in victory.

"To this day I cannot get enough of God's Word. It's a delight to seek him through his Word. I love to tell others about him. God has completely redeemed my broken past, and I have never looked back in defeat at the early tragedy that took place in my life. And I'm prepared to scream this message from the mountaintop until the day I die: God will redeem any life, save any soul, and use anybody who cooperates with him. I know because I am living proof.

"For those women struggling with childhood sexual abuse and the bondage that suffering can bring, you need to know that God doesn't simply offer an answer; he *is* the answer. If you want to know how to go from being a victim to being a victor in Christ, it's simple. Be faithful and do what God tells you to do every step of the way. It doesn't matter what state you're in, Jesus Christ wants to redeem your life. As you read God's Word, drink it in by actively and deliberately thinking, *This is what I want to be truth in my life, and I receive this, Father, by faith today.* Then ask God to make it abide in you, to make it part of you, and to make the words a reality.

"Additionally, pray that God will give you the wisdom to see the danger ahead if you don't let go of the pain associated with sexual abuse. When you are able to relinquish the pain and turn your heart fully over to Christ, you become a person God can use. The Word of God tells us in the book of Jeremiah that our heart is deceitful above all things. If your heart is not fully committed to Christ, you can't trust what you're feeling or what your heart is telling you.

"But asking Christ to give you wisdom and discernment is not a once and for all endeavor. It must be done on a daily basis. Every day of my life I wake up with needs and challenges. I have emotional needs. I often am faced with unexpected events, decisions, and possible crises. I need to know, more than anything, that I am loved. God has taught me to go to him for all of these things.

"Every day I spend time pouring out my heart to God, confessing sin that has built up in me since the previous day. This is when he begins to talk to me, to show me and convict me about my attitudes and motives—things I may be considering or situations I try to avoid because they are too painful. This is when I ask the Holy Spirit to shed light on my sins, attitudes, and motives in order to be able to walk in healing and forgiveness.

"Psalm 62 tells us we can pour out our hearts to God. He is a refuge, a safe place, for all of us. Go to him now with your pain and say, 'Lord, I want you to know that in your name, I'm going to do what you're guiding me to do to attain healing. Please come and minister to me.' And this is what you are accomplishing. You are pouring out your heart so that God can fill it with his healing. This is why it's important to start your time in prayer by emptying yourself, rather than looking to be filled.

"Continue by telling him how you feel. 'Lord, you know I am naturally given to fear. You know all my insecurities. You know that I have a need to be loved and to feel significant and to feel affirmed. But Father, you are my sole satisfaction, and I ask you to fill me this morning with your perfect love.'

"The Word of God speaks of unfailing love many times in Scripture, and it's always in reference to God's love. His is the only love that never fails. So pray to him, 'Lord, you're what I want. You are all I long for. You are the great Rewarder, the great Healer. I want your fullness in my life—not just what you can provide for me but you alone. I want you.'

"He will respond to the broken child who was wounded so long ago. He will remind you how precious you are to him. He'll say, 'Child, you are tremendously important to me. You are everything to me. I laid down my life for you. And your love for me is worth the sacrifice. Be full of my love today, and full of my Spirit. Be healed. Trust in my Word in Malachi where I say to you, "But for you who revere my name, the sun of righteousness will rise with healing in its wings"'" (Mal. 4:2).

Combating Pornography

Featuring Kathy Gallagher

"The pornography only drove him to demand more. In order to keep up with his insatiable appetite for sex, we eventually began getting sexually involved with other people."

Kathy Gallagher

PORNOGRAPHY IS DESCRIBED as a sexual addiction that creates an enslaving dependence upon erotic excitement through images or words, fantasized or real. It has infiltrated our world through a variety of sources: advertisements, adult bookstores, movies, music, literature, television, telephone sex lines, the Internet, and more. Regardless of the conduit by which it enters the marital relationship, it robs the union of intimacy, trust, purity, and emotional and physical passion.

In the United States the pornography industry is larger than the record and film industry combined and is continually on the upswing, skyrocketing out of control. Unfortunately, pornography is not absent from the body of Christ. Studies reveal that 63 percent of born-again male believers admit to struggling with pornography in the past year.[1] Two-thirds of those men are reportedly in church leadership with 10 percent being pastors. For the woman whose husband is caught in this specific web of deception, it can steal, kill, and destroy her faith, integrity, and hope. This is Kathy Gallagher's story of the struggle, the restoration, and the reconciliation she found for both her relationship with God and within her marriage.

"I grew up in a wonderful two-parent home. My parents weren't Christian, but they were moral and upright, teaching their children to be the same. My father tended to be laid back and mild in his temperament. Like clockwork he went to work in the morning and came home every night. He was reliable, but I realized looking back that even though he was physically there, emotionally he was distant. He went through a lot as a child. His father had tried to kill him several times, so to save his life he was eventually farmed out to orphanages. My mother, on the other hand, had a more direct personality.

"As a child I was extremely compliant. I wanted to please my mom and dad in the worst way. But against their better judgment, when I turned sixteen, I got married. Dee had a strong personality but, like my father, was emotionally detached.

"Dee was a prospect of the Hell's Angels and extremely abusive. In January 1979, after several years of physical abuse, I left him for good. I finally felt free—free from the tyranny of a controlling husband, free from the fear in which I had constantly lived, and free from the abuse. I had a job, my own car, and most importantly, my own life.

"Because Dee was a ruthless man and I was terrified of him, I remained incognito until things had calmed down. I eventually resumed my friendship with his older brother, Gale, and his wife, Joanne.

"I was at their home in Sacramento, California, one day when I met Steve Gallagher. I was warming myself by the heater when he came waltzing through the front door of Gale and Joanne's little shack. My first impression of him was that he seemed out of place in that environment. Steve was a real estate agent and had come to Gale's house because he was interested in selling them a new home.

"It never crossed my mind that I would someday become involved with this man. He was twenty-four, and I was only eighteen. He seemed so old to me. At any rate, as I began running into him at their house over the next few weeks, he began to pursue a relationship with me. The feelings of attraction were not mutual, and I had no desire to go out with him. Nevertheless, at Gale and Joanne's insistence, I finally agreed to a date.

"Steve picked me up in his spacious Ford LTD and whisked me off to a drive-in movie. Before we had even gotten to the movie, he expressed his desire for me to sit next to him. I informed him then that I felt no obligation to cuddle up beside a perfect stranger. So our first date ended in an argument, with me angrily storming out of his car when he finally took me home. He yelled for me to come back, which I did, and he humbly and politely suggested we start all over again.

"We continued to date over the next few weeks. One day he asked me to go with him to a beachside resort in Santa Cruz for a weekend, just the two of us. I knew what that meant: we would be in the same hotel room together for an entire weekend. This was heavy-duty. To me it meant commitment; it meant that I was giving myself to him, that I had to drop my guard and give my heart to him. I was uneasy and not sure that I was ready to take this step.

"In my mind, consenting to go was the same as saying yes to a marriage proposal. If I gave myself to him sexually, it meant that

I was his and he was mine. This wasn't just a date or a fun weekend with some guy that I liked. I had never done anything like this with anyone. Yet in some way I felt as though I was being pulled helplessly into this relationship, and I had no resistance. I finally agreed.

"We were both full of excitement and had an absolutely wonderful time. You guessed it: I fell in love with Prince Charming. When we returned home on Sunday, we immediately moved in together. I was on cloud nine at first but soon began to see what Steve was really like. Full of ambition, he worked night and day in real estate. He was bent on becoming successful, but because of his great expectations, he put undue pressure upon himself. The result was his short temper when he was home. I attributed his impatience and lack of tolerance with me to the stress of his real estate business and hoped that he would eventually change.

"Despite all of this, an interesting thing began to happen between us: Steve started to talk to me about God. He shared with me that he had first come to the Lord when he was doing jail time as a sixteen-year-old but had backslidden shortly thereafter. He said that one day he wanted to get right with God again.

"This was all news to me, but I immediately came under conviction because we had been living in sin together. Over the next few months, I lived with a sense of condemnation. I was in trouble with God, but I didn't really know what to do about it.

"Then one day I met a sweet, Southern Baptist pastor named Jess at my sister's house. He told me that I was a sinner in need of a Savior. The Lord had thoroughly prepared me for this divine appointment, and I made Jesus the Lord and Master of my life that day. The next day I packed up all my personal belongings from our home and left Steve.

"I fell in love with the Lord. I was on fire for Jesus. He became the center of my life. I spent hours reading the Word, awestruck by its profound wisdom and revelation of future events. I was in church whenever the doors opened and almost single-handedly turned that little church upside down, infecting everyone with my newfound joy. Everywhere I went I talked to others about God. People couldn't believe the changes that were happening in my life. I was a different person, literally a new creation in Christ.

"One day, zealous to see people come to know the Lord, I called Steve to try to witness to him. I wanted him to know the joy I felt, but the years of being backslidden had hardened his heart toward God. When I had left him for the Lord, he felt betrayed by God. At the end of our conversation, completely out of the blue, he told me to pray about whether we should be married. This was unthinkable! He was dead to spiritual realities, while I was alive and completely happy serving God as a single Christian. Nevertheless, over the next few weeks, his words kept ringing in my ears. I couldn't seem to escape them. In fact, I was consumed by what seemed to be a ridiculous question and found myself entertaining the thought.

"A month later, in January 1980, we were married. I had been a Christian for about five months. At first Steve began attending church with me. Little by little, though, he drifted away from God, once again unwilling to surrender to the Lord.

"Even though Steve was far more refined than my first husband, he was much more difficult to live with. He never physically abused me, but I feared him even more. Steve had a seething, violent anger that was always contained just under the surface. I saw him as the sort of person who could snap and just start killing people at random. Needless to say, he scared me.

"His anger, always directed at me, came through in his sharp, cutting tongue. He was extremely critical and sarcastic. He would ridicule me whenever I did things wrong. I could never seem to satisfy him or do anything right. This, of course, left deep, emotional wounds that hurt far more than my first husband's fists.

"In spite of this, I tried to hope for the best. I knew that much of his frustration was due in part to the fact that the real estate market had suffered a tremendous blow because of escalating interest rates. As a result, Steve's career, which he had worked so hard to establish, began to crumble. No longer able to continue in real estate, he began looking for job opportunities in law enforcement.

"Steve's job search took us to Los Angeles where he began the long, excruciating process to become a deputy sheriff. Instead of things getting better, the stress of his new job made things worse. He became even more abusive to me. Unfortunately, I sought Steve's approval rather than God's. As I became more and more consumed and obsessed with our relationship, I became weaker and more dependent on him. Gradually I, too, backslid in my faith. I would make feeble attempts to read my Bible and pray, but I had no strength or hunger inside. I had long since quit going to church.

"Not long after we moved to Los Angeles, I found out about Steve's addiction to pornography. According to Steve, it made him enjoy sex more. He gently let me know that I wasn't enough, but if we introduced porn into our marriage bed, he would be satisfied. I was crushed. I had to compete with women in pornographic movies and magazines. This was devastating to me, but instead of turning to God, I tried even harder to please Steve, agreeing to do as he requested. I longed for him to be as consumed with me as I was with him. So I intensely pursued his affection and love more than ever.

"Many days followed when I felt like my heart would literally burst from the pain and rejection I felt from my husband. Other days, usually when he was sweet to me, I held out hope that he would change. I knew that I had made a conscious decision to allow the pornography into our lives, but I had no idea at the time that it would have the opposite effect, destroying what little love we had left. I believed the lie that it would enhance our sex lives and make things better for us.

"The pornography drove Steve to demand more and more illicit sex. In order to keep up with his insatiable appetite for sex, we eventually began getting sexually involved with other people. The only way I could handle the complete loss of my own dignity and self-respect was to drown myself in drugs and alcohol. I became addicted to methamphetamine.

"After several years of doing everything I could to win Steve, I finally gave up. I had loved him so much and had been willing to do literally anything to keep him, but his obsession with illicit sex had become insane. Having lost all hope, I left him and filed for divorce. I was devastated. Not only had I lost the battle to win him, but also I had completely given up all my morals and self-respect. I had to face what I had become.

"It was then, in what appeared to me to be a miracle from God, that I met a guy named Tim. After years of emotional abuse, he was like a breath of fresh air! Immediately I forgot all the pain of being rejected by Steve. Being with him allowed me to stick my head in the sand and forget the losses I had suffered.

"Tim was so good to me. He opened car doors for me, treated me with kindness and respect, and made me laugh a lot. Unlike Steve, he was sensitive and considerate. Another thing I really appreciated was the way he would open up to me and share his heart. This never happened with either of my former husbands.

"My involvement with Tim lasted for several weeks. I began sleeping with him almost immediately, believing the deception that since we really loved each other, God would understand. Tim's continuous drinking and quick willingness to be in an adulterous relationship should have caused me to doubt his sincerity as a Christian, but I was so enthralled with him that I stifled my nagging doubts.

"I had no contact with Steve during this time, so I didn't know that when I left, he became involved with a variety of different women. One morning, unbeknownst to me, he woke up in the apartment of one of his girlfriends, feeling the emptiness of his life. All day he was miserable. That afternoon he went to work at the jail, but it was a busy evening, so he didn't get back to eat his supper in the deputy chow hall until late. There were no other deputies there when he finally arrived. As he sat there, eating in miserable silence, a deputy named Willy strolled in. He, too, was late arriving, and somehow the conversation got around to Steve's struggles. Upon hearing that Willy was a Christian, he poured out his heart to Willy, telling him how empty and unhappy he felt in life. Willy suggested that Steve give his heart to the Lord, which he did.

"'I felt like a thousand pounds lifted off my back!' Steve exclaims. 'But it didn't last long. When I got home that night, all I could think about was getting my wife back. I tossed and turned all night, upset about Kathy. In the middle of the night, I heard a voice tell me that she would call in the morning.' Steve sat, waiting by the phone for my call.

"The next morning I took Tim to work, but after dropping him off, I did a strange thing: I started driving north on the freeway toward the San Fernando Valley where Steve and I had lived. I had no idea why I was doing this; it seemed like someone else was steering the car. When I got to Van Nuys, I stopped at a phone booth and called Steve.

"He was excited to hear from me and told me what had happened the night before. I was glad to hear of his new life, but I had no intention of going back to him. My feelings for him were dead. I didn't even know why I was calling him. Why would I willingly return to him now? I now had what I wanted for so long. I was convinced that God had brought Tim into my life, and I had no desire to go back to Steve. As far as I was concerned, he had lost his opportunity, and now I felt that the Lord was restoring to me all the years that the locusts had eaten (see Joel 2:25). I was becoming accustomed to being treated like a princess. Tim was giving me the love that I had wanted from Steve; I would be a fool to return to him.

"Finally, in desperation, Steve challenged me to call my parents for their advice. It was my pleasure to call my folks. I could easily remember how furious they had become with Steve when I told them about his behavior when I left him. So I hung up the phone from him and called them. My dad answered the phone, and when I explained the situation, to my surprise, he told me that the Lord had spoken to both him and mom about me and clearly told them that I should return to my husband. Needless to say, I was in shock. Right then and there I sat down in the phone booth and cried. I didn't want to go back to him. Just the thought of doing so made my stomach turn. I finally pulled myself together and went to his apartment where Steve and I spent the night making love and talking.

"The next morning I told Steve that I needed to go get my stuff from Tim's house. He reluctantly agreed to let me go after I called

Tim's number and nobody answered. When I arrived, Tim's car was gone, but when I let myself in the house, I found him sitting on the bed. All the charm was gone now; he was furious.

"For the next two hours he angrily tried to convince me what a mistake it would be to go back to Steve. He kept badgering me, and I became confused. Tim was right. Why would I want to go back to a man who had treated me so awful for three years when I had someone who treated me so well? Tim would vacillate between calm, reasonable arguments and tirades of anger. Finally, in a rage, he ripped my blouse off and forced himself on me. I was so weak and confused at the time that I didn't even fight him off. Strangely enough, it was that act that pulled me back to Tim. The sexual union between the two of us proved to be addicting.

"At Tim's insistence, I called Steve. 'I don't love you anymore. I love Tim, and I'm not coming back,' I coldly told him. When Steve heard that, he grabbed his off-duty revolver and spun the cylinder around in the mouthpiece so I could hear it. 'All right, then you can listen to me blow my brains out!' he shouted.

"'Steve, don't do it!' I yelled. When I said that, Tim grabbed my arm firmly. I looked up at him to see the most evil look I had ever seen on anybody's face in all my life. 'Kathy, if he wants to kill himself, let him do it. It's not your fault!' It was then I realized that this man I had taken for such a prince was actually full of the devil.

"A pastor arrived at Steve's apartment about that time and picked up the phone, asking if he could pray for me. I was terrified and just wanted to get out of that house, but I was afraid to say anything. I told the pastor that I would meet him and Steve at his church and then got off the phone. At first Tim was adamant that I couldn't go, but he could see that I just wanted out of there, and finally he relented. I was so upset that I got lost driving to the church. By the time I made it to where Steve was, it had been over six hours since I'd talked with him on the phone.

"It took this experience for me to see what Tim was really like, but it didn't make going back to Steve any easier. It was difficult for a long time. The first several months I felt like I had made a huge mistake, and I was absolutely broken—broken over my sinfulness and the shame of being an adulteress but also broken because I was married to a man I no longer loved. I often felt I would rather be alone than with him. I felt my skin crawl when he touched me.

"To make matters worse, Steve was having a revival in his heart. He was on fire for the Lord and had now fallen deeply in love with me. The affection that I had wanted for so long was now mine in abundance. He constantly wanted to hold my hand and hug me and kiss me, and it made me sick. 'Why couldn't you have been like this five years ago?' I would silently exclaim. I cried many nights when I went to bed. I made sure Steve didn't know because I didn't want to hurt him, but the truth was, I just didn't want him anymore. I constantly had to fight feelings of disgust.

"Gradually, over the months, things got better. We both had so much to overcome. He retained some of the same old attitudes. There were still times he would blame-shift and manipulate and sometimes even lash out in anger. And in spite of his newfound passion for Jesus, he was also still struggling with pornography. But there was a brokenness in Steve now that had never been there before. God was winning in his life.

"It took some time for my feelings for Steve to return, but gradually they did. Actually, I think God destroyed the old foundation and built a new one, because when the Lord restored the love and respect that I had lost, it came back in a brand new way. I started to look up to and admire him more than I ever had before. There were times that my love for him became overwhelming, not in the idolatrous way it had been before but in the love of the Lord. In the years since we got back together, I have watched Steve allow God to humble him, correct him, and even crush him. Now he truly has become the man of my dreams.

"But Steve wasn't the only one who needed to change. I had to learn to put God first in my life also. This meant facing the reality that I had been just as consumed with Steve as he had been with sex. In my own self-centeredness, I had turned to one man after another, looking for fulfillment in life. I gradually learned to turn to God as the center of my life. This didn't make me love Steve less; it simply purified my love for him. Rather than a self-centered love, which was given with the ultimate goal of having my own needs met, I learned to give my husband the unselfish love of the Lord. Our marriage grew stronger and stronger.

"Almost immediately Steve and I began spending time with the Lord every morning. This set a pattern that has lasted for many years—being in touch with God daily, both individually and as a couple. This has given me a strength I had never known before. At first, as Steve continued struggling with his addiction to pornography, I became obsessed with his deliverance, policing his every move. God quietly began convicting me and kept leading me back to himself. I soon discovered that the more connected I was with God, the more strength I had to help Steve with his problems. I went from trying to fix Steve myself, to allowing God to do his work in Steve's heart.

"As I continued to grow in the Lord, I was able to recognize the good that came from failure instead of seeing it as a catastrophe.

Because Steve was serious about his life with God, each fall back into sin served as a blessing in disguise. It deepened the hatred of sin in his heart. Instead of falling apart when he would fail, I became an encouragement through those failures. The desire to be supportive of his efforts in this struggle and to keep him accountable in a loving way grew stronger.

"There was a time when I did not have the maturity or emotional strength to help bear his burdens in this way, but the closer I got to the Lord, the more I was able to handle. I came to realize that as long as Steve (or his victory) held the center stage of my heart, my joy would fall to pieces every time he failed. As I increasingly allowed God the throne of my heart, I found that I now had new strength to help my husband through his failures.

"Steve had one last struggle with sexual immorality in the summer of 1985. After that, it took us some time to realize it, but Steve was finally free. This is when things really began to change in our lives. I could actually start leaning on him and confessing my faults to him. We reversed roles: he became my spiritual head, and I became a wife who could submit to her leader with joy.

"What a relief it was when I finally realized I no longer had to look over my shoulder. I still had to continue to repent of my own suspicious nature, but in my heart I knew we had crossed the deep waters of sexual addiction together. In our relationship, we have a depth that few enjoy.

"Trusting God by going back to Steve was a turning point in my life, but it was also only the beginning of my own restoration. The restoration of our marriage came about because we both wanted God more than we wanted each other or our own desires.

"This year Steve and I celebrate twenty-three years of marriage. It was only a year after Steve's last fall in sin in the summer of 1985 that God laid the burden on his heart to begin Pure Life Ministries to help other men out of sexual bondage. You know God has done a work in your heart when he takes your failures and entrusts you to help others with theirs.

"Since that time our love for God has intensified and our love for each other has deepened. What God has given me has been worth all of the grief I have endured through the years, not because of my happy marriage but because of what I have in the Lord. Overall, what I've realized is that there is no pit so deep that the love of God isn't deeper.

"God really has restored the years eaten away by the locust but not the way I originally thought he would. Don't be misled; it hasn't been easy, but it's definitely been worth it. Steve and I both had to learn to trust in the Lord that he could change us individually, then as a couple. Hebrews 11:6 affirms this when it says, 'And without faith it is impossible to please God, because anyone who comes to him must believe that he exists and that he rewards those who earnestly seek him.'"

Married to the Ministry

Featuring Jill Briscoe

"There was only one problem with this mission field: me. I was not the teacher God wanted me to be, and for a simple reason: I could not control my temper."

Jill Briscoe

HAVE YOU A "BESETTING SIN," one area of weakness in your life that is weak forever? We all seem to. I think about Moses. He had a fiery temper. He demonstrated it from his watery coffin by screaming in baby tantrums at the crocodiles. It manifested itself in cold-blooded fury when, after carefully "glancing this way and that way" (see Exod. 2:12), he murdered the Egyptian who was tormenting his Hebrew brother. He proved its dominion over him when he descended down from the mountain having seen God face-to-face. Finding the naked, idolatrous worshippers, he lost his cool completely by literally breaking the Ten Commandments! Was it desperation or temper that caused him to sin by smiting the rock twice? Yes, it certainly appeared that Moses had a besetting sin.

I always believed in God, that Jesus Christ was his Son, and that the Bible was true. And my parents went out of their way to teach me the difference between right and wrong. It was put in silent yet simplistic terms: right was being "good," which would make me and everyone else happy; wrong was being "bad," which would make me and everyone else sad. What no one really expressed to me, perhaps out of lack of information or ignorance, was why I found myself with the desire to be bad instead of good.

I've always been self-analytical, examining the cognitive process that I take myself through a thousand times a day. As a child I had much to indulge my mind. Education, recreation, travel, friendships, wholesome entertainment, a loving family, and carefree days were at my beck and call. And while I enjoyed them immensely, I found myself being unsatisfied and wanting more.

Like Eve, I didn't realize that the process of death begins with the first bite from the forbidden tree of life. So, while I knew I shouldn't read dirty books growing up, I compromised my sin and indulged in inappropriate thoughts that could be hidden behind my smile. I'd been told it was wrong to cheat at exams, but I could dispense with my guilt by arguing that cheating made for better grades, and better grades for happier parents—as long as I wasn't caught! But even if I was, I would chloroform my conscience and lie myself out of a situation, which I reasoned would be kinder than telling the truth, which would cause hurt and embarrassment to those I love.

These sinful examples may seem silly, but they were instrumental in forming a shifting foundation of selfishness that would later prove to be detrimental in my heart. They taught me how to manipulate, present a façade, and overall, how to lie behind a smile. So it was no surprise, looking back, that God had a plan to strip me of the desires of self and bring me into loving submission to his will for my life.

This transformation began to make itself real to me when I was eighteen. I had come to the conclusion that if I left my current environment the answers would fall into place. My chance came to prove the point when I was accepted at a teachers' training college at Cambridge.

"Yes," I lied to the interviewer, "I love little children." The truth was that I'd never given it much thought. I was self-consumed and soon found upon acceptance to the college that children were a nuisance to me. They made demands on my precious, trivia-filled time that I so cherished. So I began a trek to find the answer to fill the void inside of me that left me questioning everyone and everything.

I majored in drama and art, which helped me to project the smile and perform whatever role it suited my selfish interest to play. My life now became like one long play, in every sense of the word. Before the curtains drew back and revealed me, I was alone, frightened, unsure of how I would relate to the crowd. It was terribly important to me to know that I pleased them. Back in the dressing room with the makeup off, the costumes laid aside, what exhaustion, depression, and unfulfilled feelings were mine!

About that time, for no apparent reason, I came down a with a mysterious stomach ailment that hospitalized me. Behind the smile I was terrified. No longer was my major concern to fill a selfish life or get my own way but to deal with fear, cope with pain, look at the suffering of others, and find a relevant comforting word. I was forced to grapple with the reality of death and find an answer.

In God's graciousness, I discovered that when I was flat on my back, there was only one way to look. Up! "Help!" I said. "Make me better. Get me out of here! Quick, stop the pain. Are you hearing me?" He did, placing a great transmitter next to my left ear.

Her name was Jenny, and she lay in the bed next to mine. She told me I had a snake in my garden, that I'd listened to his every word and believed his lies instead of God's truth. The result was that I'd ended up conceited and arrogant. I'd been my own god, but now I couldn't even answer my own prayers. No wonder I was sick in my soul. My sin found me wearing fig-leaf arguments, carefully stitched but painfully inadequate.

"Jesus came and died on the cross for you, Jill," Jenny told me. "There he bruised the serpent's head and defeated him but not before the snake had bruised his heel so that he suffered dreadfully. He rose again triumphant over death and sin and is alive. He wants to come into your life by his Holy Spirit."

"What's the Holy Spirit?" I asked. I had heard of the Holy Ghost, but his name had conjured up a picture of a sheet-shrouded spook who haunted old English churches! In my ignorant opinion he was left free to do so because evidently God had either died or gone on vacation, leaving behind his ghostly janitor.

"The Holy Spirit was his divine nature released at Pentecost," she explained. "The Holy Spirit makes it possible for you to possess the very life of Christ."

Her words penetrated my empty soul. The smile forgotten, tears flowed as, exposed to my sin, I accepted God's covering for my nakedness. Clothed in his forgiveness and his grace, I turned around to walk away from disobedience to a new life.

Jenny discipled me from her hospital bed, and we spent many hours talking about who Jesus was and what he wanted to do in our lives. "Here you are in the hospital," Jenny said, encouraging me one day, "You think you have been laid aside by illness, but you haven't. You've been called aside for stillness. So get your nose in the Bible and start."

After a couple of weeks longer in the hospital, I was released. I went back to college and graduated, becoming a teacher in my hometown of Liverpool, England. I taught first graders, loved my work, and had plenty of free time for serving the Lord. I learned so much about my relationship with God during this time. Someone once said, "The mission field is between your own two feet." If that were true, part of my commission lay within the four walls of my classroom. "First graders?" I asked myself one day. Well, they surely needed a changed nature, sweet though they were! I never had to teach them to answer back, be rude, selfish, or stubborn; all that appeared to come quite naturally.

There was only one problem with this mission field: me. I was not the teacher God wanted me to be and for a simple reason: I could not control my temper. On several occasions I would kneel at home and ask forgiveness, knowing that inappropriate anger had to be beaten in my life. How could I serve him when a part of my life was constantly being defeated? Sin had become my master in this area of my heart. Miserable, I struggled to gain control over my temper at school. Day after day I returned defeated to pray the same prayer, "Forgive me, Lord, I did it again." *If there was no victory in the Christian life, just what did Christ offer?* I wondered.

At that time I read a story about a lighthouse keeper who broke a window in his lighthouse. Believing no ships were in the area, he filled in the aperture with a board. The light shone brightly from all sides except one. There was only one part dark. Surely it wouldn't matter. That night a ship approaching the lighthouse on the dark side was shipwrecked. The moral: There must be no dark part. I knew this. No matter how much his light was shining out of other areas of my life, this temper part was dark; it was tripping up those to whom I was seeking to witness at school.

As I worked on creating balance in this area of my life, I reasoned that perhaps what I needed was a husband to help me. I quickly dismissed this thought, afraid that God might present me with a balding, squint-eyed, spotty boy six inches shorter than me and say, "He's a great Christian; marry him!" No, it was much safer to forget about marriage. The obvious thing for me to do in my mind was to head for Africa and become an intrepid missionary. There I could bury myself beneath a jungle hat and a mosquito net and deal with my struggle silently. So I applied to Bible college and waited for acceptance that never came.

In the meantime, I decided to spend time seeking to disciple a wild group of teenagers who had found Christ through a local ministry. I found myself with eighty teens. They were hungry, baby Christians, eager to learn all I could teach them. This didn't take long, so I looked around for direction. All the people I asked advised me to take them away for a retreat. So away we went to a beautiful castle, Capernwray Hall, situated at the gateway to England's Lake District. It was a Christian youth conference center run by an organization called Torchbearers. There I found freedom with discipline, fun without frivolity—in other words, balance. Here I watched the gifted staff counsel and teach, encourage and train my young people. And here I met a man who was used by God to bring balance to me.

Stuart Briscoe was tall, dark, and handsome, so obviously he was a temptation sent by the devil to distract me from following the Lord, I reasoned. Never in those first days did it occur to me that God could give me a man like this. One evening while battling with my vulnerable heart, I read that Jesus sent his disciples out two by two!

"Don't tease me, Lord," I prayed. "You know my heart. You know I'm happy alone with you. So what's happening to me?" "Step into my plan for your life, Jill," he whispered. So I did and married Stuart, learning that weddings last a day but marriage is forever.

My temper still existed. It did not go away because I ignored it. Instead, it lay dormant within my heart as I walked in ministry, raising its ugly head within me from time to time. I'd smile and stuff the anger that boiled up inside of me. But that was not good enough for God. He wanted healing, and he would get it so that he might be glorified. Boy, was I in for an unexpected adventure!

Right after we got married, Stuart was given two missions to choose from. One of them offered the opportunity for us to be together and do some ministry. The other one meant that he would be working with the armed forces in Europe and would have to be gone all the time, so we picked the first choice. A year into that decision, Stuart was asked to plant a mission worldwide, a job that he was unable to do from home. Suddenly, he was gone ten months out of the year.

There was absolutely no question in both our minds that we were in the right place and this was what God wanted us to do. So we went forward with the opportunity for Stuart to expand worldwide missions.

Right after this job change I began to feel the anger rise up within my life again. I had just given birth to our first child. As I happily washed, cooked, worked, and cared for our newborn, a lie was whispered to me from the enemy, Satan. He was misquoting Scripture, but it sounded familiar to me, so I was taken off guard.

"It is not good for the man to be alone," he hissed in my ear. "God never intended it, so why does that Christian husband leave you alone so much? He should be here to help you with the baby and the work instead of being busy with God's business!" I had forgotten that this verse referred to the man and that the woman was created to help the man, not vice versa.

The fruit of self-pity looked good to me, so I ate it. It immediately created a desire in me to encourage my husband to eat it also.

"Why don't you stay home on the weekends and evangelize here?" I asked him. "Look over there outside that Cat's Whisker coffee bar across the street. All those young people need to hear the gospel. Why preach to a dozen little old ladies in church?"

Now let me assure you, I could not have cared less about the needy young people across the street. I was simply using them as an excuse to get my own way. I was lonely, and so I was manipulating to get Stuart to obey me rather than God. And I was using a religious excuse to accomplish my purpose. How true is Scripture that says, "The heart is deceitful above all things and beyond cure" (Jer. 17:9).

Looking out of our windows and across the street, my husband commented simply, "Why do you think you are here? You reach them."

A thousand excuses leaped to my lips. "My job is to be your wife and look after you and the baby while praying and supporting your ministry. I haven't time!"

"Well, you have more time than I have," he replied. "Jill, God doesn't ask you for your husband's time or your child's time; he asks you for your spare time!" And with this he packed his case and was gone.

The struggle would continue as I realized that even though I had committed my life to Stuart, this did not mean I had committed my relationship with God to Stuart! That was still my responsibility. Even though we could read and pray and learn of him together, even though God had a special plan for our lives collectively, I needed to fulfill his plan for my life individually. I needed to guard my own personal devotional time and not let collective devotions take that place.

It was a new beginning for both of us. I sat down and made a note of my daily routine and blocked off my spare time, setting it aside for God. Our home could be my fishing boat during Stuart's absence. Our baby could be a means of contact among other young mothers in the park or at the store. I had a commission from God not only to care physically and practically for my family's needs in a manner that would bring glory to him but also to bring the gospel to every creature. I must not abdicate that responsibility just because I had gotten married.

I began a youth outreach ministry that over time would grow as days passed into months and months into years in various places. Stuart's ministry developed and took him away for increasing amounts of time. Having once dealt with my resentful heart about the issue of his absence, I didn't expect to have to deal with it again. I learned the hard way. Victory won yesterday does not mean victory automatically dispensed for the rest of life.

Although I kept myself thoroughly involved and saw much blessing, once more I began to fall prey to discontentment and self-pity. I read the story of Mary's little alabaster box of ointment. I believe Jewish girls kept these treasured boxes of ointment as security. They were their "marriage boxes." If they never married, the precious ointment would provide for them. If they did marry, the proceeds would be part of their parental provision. They were, as the Bible says, "very precious." So was mine!

My "marriage box" again became more valuable than my relationship with my Lord and Savior Jesus Christ. I was amazed at how hypocritical I could be, pretending all was well yet knowing differently. I watched my senior missionaries and tried to copy their ways. I learned to wave my husband off on a three-month tour with just the right evangelical smile. With a false earnestness which apparently was believed, I mouthed the usual pious platitudes to those who sympathized over our separation. "Oh, the Lord will look after us. Don't worry. He will give us the peace we need and make it all up to us in some way," I assured them. Now this was true, and I knew it, but I was frosting up solidly on the inside. The warmth of the Lord's provision was far from my experience. The problem was that I didn't want his help. I wanted my husband!

I stopped reading the Bible—it was far too relevant—and I stopped praying. After all, I had nothing to say and certainly didn't want to hear his voice any more. Why, the last time I'd turned to the Word for comfort, my eyes had been drawn to the words, "Is it not lawful for me to do what I will with mine own?" (Matt. 20:15 KJV).

"It may be 'lawful,'" I snapped, shutting my Bible, "but I think it is awful!"

At this point in my spiritual experience, I hadn't learned that his rod and staff comfort the stupid wayward sheep. I didn't like the prods one little bit, nor did I appreciate his staff reaching down into my hole of depression to get me out. Depression suited me much better. As the enemy fed me multiple reasons to be angry, I spent several dreadful weeks contemplating my mistrust of God's ways.

"Don't give in," the enemy whispered. "If you do, you know he won't let Stuart stay at home; he'll just take Stuart away all the more! Stand up for your rights! Let your husband know how unhappy you are. You know how to do that, don't you? When he says, 'Is anything wrong, dear?' say 'No, nothing' in such a way that he knows perfectly well there is!"

I knew exactly what he was talking about and knew how well I could do just that. I was appalled as I realized the power I had as a Christian wife. I could so easily make my husband worry about me. I could hinder or even prevent him from obeying God! Standing up for my rights couldn't mean that! The enemy had overstepped himself again, and I suddenly recognized the source of my thoughts. I began to open up the lines of communication with God again.

"You don't know what it is like being so lonely, Lord," I accused him.

"My Son once left home for more than thirty years!" he replied.

"Well," I countered, "you don't know what it is like to be separated. You were with him in spirit."

The shadow of the cross and the voice of one crying, "My God, My God, Why hast thou forsaken me?" (Matt. 27:46 KJV) was his answer. "Jill, it was your sin, all that rebellion and self-pity and anger, that separated me from my Son. I punished him instead of you because I love you, and because I love you, I want you to believe that! My will for your life is good and perfect and *acceptable.*"

My disobedience had so numbed my feelings that my heart couldn't believe that his will could be acceptable. Endurable, yes, but not acceptable! However, I could apply my mind and my will to respond. I needed to start reading the Bible again even though I knew I would read things that would convict and condemn me.

I began where I had left off, the story of Mary's little box. I fought a battle with my pride. I knew I should go and seek counsel from my senior missionary. She was one who had obviously yielded her marriage box years before and apparently was enjoying happiness and victory.

The enemy did not relent on bombarding my mind. "Just imagine her face," he shrieked. "How can you bear to let her know you are a failure? Keep up appearances. Nobody needs to know your heart's condition!" I thought of Mary. How hard it must have been for her to bring her "marriage box" out in front of all those people and give it to Jesus. Everyone knew the disciples had left all to follow him, and here she was with an unyielded box! What would they say? It would be much better to keep it hidden. She knew Jesus would never take it from her by force. Surely it was enough to sit at his feet, listen to his word, entertain him in her home, and keep her little box hidden and intact.

At last I went and talked with the senior missionary. I discovered the breakage of her little alabaster box had been as difficult in her experience as mine. She was loving and sympathetic but firm with me.

"Jill, you've given God everything except this one little box; and it doesn't matter whether it's a marriage box or a box of another sort, holding back anything is backsliding. You'll never move one step forward, never hear his Word in your heart, never see an answer to prayer when there is known disobedience in your life!"

I thought about Achan's sin in Joshua 7. Buried deep within his tent was the treasure Achan thought no one knew about! But God knew. No depth of earth can hide the precious things we seek to conceal in disobedience. They only spoil, hidden within the cold earth.

I, like Achan, knew my disobedience would bring trouble to my loved ones and to God's people. No more victories could be won until all had been exposed.

Washing his feet with my tears, I spilled ointment and prayed, "Oh, God, stop me from trying to scrape this up and put it back in the box again!"

"People will come to know about me because of the aroma," God replied.

A miracle had occurred in my heart. My pain and offering was acceptable to God.

Over the following years as Stuart traveled worldwide, I developed a youth warehouse ministry that exceeded even our highest expectations. God was moving in new ways and was faithful in the harvest.

There came a time after the initial establishing of the warehouse that I found myself tired out physically and somewhat depressed. Metaphorically speaking, I was like King David. At a time when kings should have been going forth to battle, I was staying home. As an old Chinese proverb says, "You can't stop the birds from flying over your head, but you can stop them from nesting in your hair!" That's true. The eggs were laid, and the young were hatched in my hair before I lifted a finger to do anything about it!

It happened at a meeting of all places. There I was sitting on the front row in a packed room listening to my husband preaching a most powerful message on Abraham. Suddenly, without any warning, the enemy of my soul whispered, "Have you forgotten he's going away tomorrow for three months? You should be at home packing, comforting your poor children, and praying for yourself!" I tried to ignore him. After all, Stuart's voice was loud enough to drown him out. But he entangled himself around my Bible and tried to distract me. What was he doing? Well, he was actually preaching his own sermon from my husband's text!

He was saying to me, "It's all right for Abraham. He was just like your husband. Look at him up there, all that faith oozing out. He's going off tomorrow to a land he 'knows not of' and will no doubt do great exploits for God. But what about Isaac? That's you!"

As soon as I began to give my full attention to the snake's interpretation of the passage, I was in trouble. I shut off the preacher and turned on the snake! And I did it all "behind the smile"!

As I walked home, I began voluntarily to wallow in a sea of self-pity. The snake was right. What about poor old Isaac? It was all right for Abraham, but it was Isaac who was bound upon the altar and would feel the knife! The same old struggle began; the snake was attacking the same old weak spot. The future, husbandless and lonely, stretched before me. My frustration grew. This had been yielded before. If the Bible said I was dead to sin, why was I leaping off the altar of sacrifice at this moment of time and feeling very much alive?

This was to be Stuart's last night at home before the journey that would take him to the primitive mission fields of the world. There he would help minister to hundreds of missionaries who were tired and dry, having had no opportunity for spiritual food for months, perhaps even years. I thought about Isaac and how he had managed to acquiesce to God's plan for his life: he must have chosen to die. He was not a little boy but in all probability a grown teenager. He must have submitted himself trustingly to his father's will, no matter how fearful he was. He must have believed they would both "come again" to the men who were waiting a little way off. In other words, he believed that life would come through death!

This was my choice. I had to get back on that altar and stay there. By the time Stuart returned, weary and ready to pack his bag and get to sleep, the battle was won. I didn't know it then, but this was to be the last long period of separation for us for a while. I'm so glad I made it back to the altar.

Shortly after Stuart's three-month trip, he nonchalantly asked me, "How would you like to be a pastor's wife? A church in America has invited me to be their pastor." We had had such invitations before but had never really seriously considered them. We both had felt his ministry belonged to the world. Why limit Stuart to one church and leave the wonderful worldwide opportunities he was being given?

For the next few weeks we received correspondence and phone calls from the leaders of this church, reaffirming their conviction that they believed it God's will that we should come.

"We're going to have to pray about it!" said Stuart cheerfully as he set off for another three-month preaching tour.

At this point I found it difficult to pray from a neutral position. By now Stuart and I were separated for nine months of the year, and I had needed all my prayers to give me the power to stop crawling off the altar! With the possibility of more time together on the horizon, it became difficult to pray, "Thy will be done," and mean it. Everything inside of me wanted so desperately for us to be together as a family.

"Please, Lord, give me the answer soon," I pleaded. "I don't think I can stay willing to your will for very long!"

There were more reasons for wanting to go than the important personal need of a normal marital situation. For quite a while I had felt a sense of completion where the youth work was concerned. It was as if my job was finished, and I had worked myself out of a job. My coworker had confided in me that she was strangely burdened and called to involve herself full-time in this ministry. She could easily assume the leadership if there were someone to take her place. And it just so "happened" that there was!

Our children were the biggest factor of all. I felt I had failed in so many ways to be both father and mother to them, especially to our oldest son, David, who was by now twelve years old. It was obvious he needed a man around. Our little girl, Judy, was also beginning to display signs of insecurity. I turned to the Word for support in my decision and prayed, asking the Shepherd of my children to lead Stuart and me in the right path where his little lambs were concerned and sought special instructions.

Sitting on a beautiful English hillside beside a rushing, bubbling stream, I perused the Gospel of John. Approaching the end of the book, I still didn't feel I had received any directive.

I pleaded, "Lord, help me to go on reading until I sense your direction. You promised to show me the right path. Is it the right thing to do to put the children first this time? Please tell me." Continuing to read in John 21, I came to the question asked by the Lord, "Do you love me?" That was worth thinking about. Yes, I did love him, even though my love was weak and poor. As Peter answered, so did I, "Lord, you know my heart. I am fond of you!" Then he asked me as he asked Peter long ago, "Do you truly love me more than these?" More that what? Than Stuart, than my homeland of England, my children, and my people? More than these?

I replied, "You know all things, Lord; I love you a little, and I want to love you more. I would like to think I love you first." I think the Shepherd smiled. Anyway, he gave me my answer: "Keep your love for me the most important thing in your life. 'Seek first his kingdom and his righteousness, and all these things will be given to you as well' (Matt. 6:33). And now you will be shown the right path in this instance."

"*Feed my lambs.*" There was my answer! It was repeated twice for emphasis. "My lambs," he had said. I knew who he was talking about: our children. He was telling me that they were his concern, and he had the best in mind for them. He had planned them in love. Seeing the birth of resentment in their hearts before I had ever noticed it, he had moved to make it possible for us to have the period of their growing teenage years together!

I ran down the hillside back to our home. I put a call through to Stuart in New York to tell him what the Lord had been revealing. My husband had left home feeling unconvinced about the wisdom of a move. But as he sat in New York in a big convention meeting the very night I called him, the preacher used a verse that convinced him of God's guidance about our decision. It was Deuteronomy 32:30, which says, "One [of you will] chase a thousand, and two put ten thousand to flight" (NASB). We were going to work together, and what was more we were going to "live" together—how exciting and challenging! We wired the church, accepting the call. Now all I had to do was pack up and be ready to move.

The enemy plays on our weaknesses. He is not a gentleman! He delights in kicking us when we are down and is neither sorry nor sympathetic. He hates us. He would destroy us if he could; and because he can't, he would render us desperate and inoperative by continually attacking our main area of weakness. At times, being aware of his devices doesn't even help. We can be fully aware of what he is doing; but after saying no for weeks, months, or even years, there can come a time when we say yes. Perhaps we are lax in our relationship with God or lazy in our service. Maybe we are like King David who was caught "looking" and forgot to bring "every thought" into captivity to Christ.

Looking back, I muse over "dying" to my flesh! Sometimes it's such a battle. One of the toughest lessons I've learned is that the way to up is down, and the way to life is death. You see, the Word of God is truth, and we must die to ourselves to grow in Christ. John 12:24 says it best: "Unless a kernel of wheat falls to the ground and dies, it remains only a single seed. But if it dies, it produces many seeds."

Sexual Dysfunction in Marriage

Featuring Joyce Penner

"I learned and internalized a belief that sex was wrong based on the interaction of my parents with each other."

Joyce Penner

IN 1999, a national survey of people between the ages of eighteen and fifty-nine showed that sexual dysfunction among women was common. To be specific, research showed that 60 to 70 percent of women do not have an orgasm during intercourse. Further information indicates that 43 percent of women have a decreased desire to be intimate with their mate.

A woman's sex drive is guided by a complex system of signals between the brain, the ovaries, and other reproductive sexual organs. A healthy brain, over a healthy body, dictates a woman's desire for sex. Any disruption in this complex interaction may cause a woman to be less interested in sex or have the inability to reach an orgasm.

There are many different types of sexual dysfunction, including a lack of interest in sex, known as decreased libido; the inability to attain or maintain adequate vaginal lubrication and a swelling response, known as female sexual arousal disorder; painful intercourse, known as dyspareunia; painful, involuntary contractions of the vaginal muscles, known as vaginismus; and a delay or absence of orgasm.

Sexual dysfunction in women rarely has a single cause. Some causes of dysfunction may include a neurological disorder, pelvic surgery or trauma, side effects of drugs, chronic kidney disease, illegal drug use, previous traumatic sexual experience, or a history of incest or molestation.

Some women, however, without medical or psychological issues, have difficulty reaching an orgasm or struggle with a decrease in libido. Sometimes this can be due to congestion in the mind stemming from childhood core beliefs about sex or intimacy. Joyce Penner, a licensed therapist and nurse, is a specialist in the field of sexual dysfunction. She and her husband, Cliff, have traveled all over the world helping couples obtain a more fulfilling sexual relationship. Even more intriguing is her own story about how her sexuality was formed from her own childhood beliefs and experiences. This is her story about how she overcame sexual hurdles in her own life and how others can do the same.

"I was raised in a Mennonite home where we lived simply in a small farming community of 611 people. We were a close-knit community with the majority of people in town being direct relatives to one another. It was a safe, loving, and warm place to grow up.

"Although we were an open and free-spirited group of individuals, certain things were not talked about in common circles, and sex was one of them. As it should be, it fell on the shoulders of the parents to educate their children on intimacy and sexual intercourse as they grew and developed as sexual persons. But because sex was not talked about in my home, there was no verbal message that sex was a God-designed gift to man and woman. So I had to learn my core beliefs about sex by nonverbal cues, the example of my parents. What I learned indirectly was that sex was an anxious thing.

"I was a free-spirited child, mainly because I felt safe in this little rural community and there was such a large extended family. We would get together on Sundays, and we'd go to church in the morning, then have dinner at noon at one of our family member's homes. After supper, the kids would go out to play, and the adults would visit. This is where I received my first experience with sexual intrigue. We were curious and would be creative and experimental with one another. There was no molestation but normal curiosity and interest about how God had made little boys and girls different.

"So there I was, a free-spirited young child getting an education about identity and learning, indirectly, how I was different than the opposite sex. As I moved into adolescence and started developing, my mother gave me a positive message about becoming a woman. I received good preparation for menstruating, wearing a bra, and maturing into womanhood. I received affirmation in a loving, warm, nurturing home that development and change was just part of life and something that every woman experiences. Looking back, I can see that when it came to male-female interaction, I had a lot of tension within me.

"Sometimes we learn by watching the interaction between other males and females. For me, it was my parents. A couple of different situations led to an insecurity and lack of confidence when interacting with the opposite sex that would be later defined as my sexuality.

"I was probably a freshman in high school when a bunch of us kids went together to the next town to a fair. It was just a group of kids in the car and nothing one on one. When I came home, my mother was intensely upset about what I had potentially done or what I had been doing. She had assumed that I had been doing something inappropriate with a boy. But I wasn't. Her accusations and anger left me confused because I didn't understand why she was upset or what I possibly had done wrong. I was so naïve and unaware that she was functioning out of her own beliefs about sexual interaction that all I received in my spirit was confusion and a sense that it wasn't safe to have fun and enjoy myself in mixed company.

"In addition to that experience, I learned and internalized a belief that sex was wrong based on the interaction of my parents with each other. My dad was one to tease and flirt with my mom, sometimes by coming up behind her and putting his arms around her shoulders or by touching her lovingly. But by her reaction, she made clear that she was uncomfortable, giving the impression that 'we shouldn't be doing this.'

"It's important for children to see positive, loving interactions between their parents. Kids act like they hate it when their dad kisses their mom, but it teaches them that it's OK to love someone freely and that it breeds intimacy in a couple. In retrospect I can see that the type of interaction my parents had pushed a button in my mother that brought fear, a feeling she didn't know how to address. So from that fear, my mother would become accusatory against my sister and me and because she didn't know how to address it and talk about it, we would sometimes get into trouble because of her assumptions that something had happened between us and a boy.

"Part of my mother's response came from her own upbringing. She thought she'd done well to teach us about being a woman because nobody had ever taught her about menstruation or other normal developmental stages of a woman's life. And while she did a good job in that area, sexual interaction and intimacy were two areas that she was incapable of passing on to us girls. Those experiences, with the absence of teaching about male-female interaction, had a drastic affect on my ability to interact with the opposite sex in a platonic or intimate relationship.

"Additionally, there were a number of unspoken rules within our community, one of which was that the Mennonites were not to date non-Mennonites. Since most of the young adults in my town were my first or second cousins, there was a strong chance that anyone I'd be interested in likely wouldn't be Mennonite. So part of the conflict and fear of my mother was an interest I verbalized to date outside of my community.

"In conjunction with this, I too experienced fear about having an attraction or becoming involved with someone who was the whole extreme of being unequally yoked. As a result, when I found myself attracted to someone who wasn't a Mennonite, I felt a lot of tension and guilt. So, while it was an unspoken rule of the community, it was an issue that was never addressed, so the feelings I had that were associated with dating outside of my community were internalized.

"This fear, guilt, and confusion stirred within my body and left me feeling insecure, not knowing how to handle relationships with guys. So I subconsciously taught myself that in order to avoid conflict with my mother or within myself, I just needed to avoid boys. I went to great lengths to make sure a boy didn't ask me out and never formally went out on a date during high school.

"When I was a junior in high school, I developed strong feelings toward a guy. He liked me too, and I knew he was going to ask me out. I struggled with so much internal turmoil over this situation that I got a fever and actually developed an infection that led to strep throat and rheumatic fever. It's easy to say, 'Joyce, there was a legitimate medical reason for getting sick,' but I think a lot of it was psychosomatic. Some of the problem was pychogenic; after all, I was ultimately diagnosed with an illness, but it's clear to me that my body was actually reacting to the amount of anxiety and fear I was experiencing. Sickness was a convenient way for me to avoid my feelings, and in some ways, opportune for my mom's fears for me not to be available to boys. While I believe that the sickness was not directly related to my internal chaos, it was encouraged or nurtured in some way because of the conflict around my sexuality.

"When I went away to college to attend an all-Mennonite school, a funny thing happened. That free-spirited, young, carefree girl from my childhood returned. Now that I was out of my parents' home and in an environment where I felt comfortable, that inner child came back. It felt good to be in a place where I could enjoy my extended family of the Mennonite community. The rule at this college was that we couldn't date during the first nine weeks, but we could walk around the block. So I took advantage of this opportunity, released my anxiety and fear, and walked around the block with a different guy almost every night. It was a good experience for me to learn how to interact with the opposite sex in a nonsexual sort of way.

"My God-given vibrancy and intensity of sexuality came back even though I didn't acknowledge it as sexuality. And that's when I met my husband Cliff. After a couple of months of dating, Cliff kissed me, and I ended up in the hospital for two weeks with an undiagnosed illness! Those feelings of anxiety and fear were still there, only suppressed.

"Those feelings of guilt and confusion returned when I was in the hospital and my parents came to visit me. During their visit Cliff showed up and sat on the edge of my bed. My parents got really upset. They thought it was inappropriate for him to sit on the edge of the bed. Their imaginations soared, and their perception of our relationship was distorted. But Cliff hadn't done anything wrong. He too had been raised in a Mennonite home. But because he didn't get as much fear instilled in him as a young boy, he was much more confident, assertive, and outgoing about his identity and dating than I was.

"Cliff and I dated for four years on and off again (mostly on), which gave us the opportunity to date other people. It was good for me to have this experience before we settled with each other because I'd never dated before Cliff. After continuing to date each other, we decided to get engaged. Cliff and I had both committed to abstinence, so we didn't have sex until our wedding night.

"When we became engaged, I was attending the Baptist School of Nursing in St. Paul, Minnesota. During the last semester there, we had a clinical psychologist on staff who was a vital part of my education. She was a strong Christian woman, and during the last semester she taught a preparation of marriage class. As part of that study, she taught about sexual adjustment in marriage. Her lessons were taught from a good biblical perspective, and I received healthy affirmations as a Christian woman. I just soaked it in because I was so naïve.

"I remember watching the first sex education film as a freshman in nursing and just watching wide-eyed, taking it all in. To my surprise it didn't make me feel bad, but instead, freed my fear, anxiety, and confusion, replacing it with good biblical understanding. Cliff was at Bethel College just a few miles from where I was in school, so I would take notes, and we would meet in the evenings, talking and discussing what I had learned. I am convinced that, with the boundaries we had in place, this helped us get our sex life off to a great start after we were married. It was then that we learned about what was appropriate and inappropriate in a Christian marriage according to God's Word. We also learned to appreciate each other as sexual beings that God created us to be. As a result, later in our marriage, Cliff and I wrote the book, *Getting Your Sex Life Off to a Great Start,* which has been instrumental in helping thousands of newlywed couples. It is the only marriage book that systematically and carefully prepares the engaged couple for their sexual relationship in marriage. Additionally, it prepares them for intimacy in marriage, which is so much more than just sex. It's how to be open with each other, how to share spiritually and emotionally. It's examining what you learned and what was modeled in your home. Further, the couple examines their expectations and learns to reclarify them to apply them appropriately to marriage.

"Initially, as we explored each other as a newlywed couple, we struggled with learning that sex was OK to engage in and that intimacy was a natural, not shameful thing. We took this opportunity to pray and read Scripture together, spending the first year of marriage learning everything the Bible says about sex and intimacy. Knowing that my sexuality was important not only to my husband but also to God who had created me made me confident in my expression of my feelings.

"As a result, I became much freer in expressing my sexuality to Cliff, learned to develop trust, and eventually found comfort with sex and my identity as a sexual person. We are passionate with each other as a married couple. We had a lot of desire for each other when we were dating. We had drawn boundaries, and we did pretty good, but it was no secret that we were passionately attracted to each other. Without setting boundaries ahead of time, it could have easily turned into unbridled passion and caused more guilt and anxiety later in our union. But we adhered to the boundaries we had set because we respected each other. That respect helped set a good foundation for when we were married.

"Many times in marriage one or both partners have unrealistic expectations about the sexual relationship. Media further complicates things, giving us the implicit message that sex in marriage is something that happens to you rather than the truth, which is that you can be intentional and deliberate and that you are responsible for making your sex life great. A good sex life is choosing to be deliberate about it by doing the preparation and work you need to do.

"One of the expectations many couples have is that sex is something that just zaps us. That's one reason there is so much sex outside of marriage. These couples act like sex is something out of their control, but it's not. You have a choice, and you can be intentional and deliberate about it. Some newlyweds, filled with the adrenaline of the new sexual relationship, struggle when it wears off. Research shows that the time will come sometime between the six- and thirty-month time period, and if the transition is not made from newness passion into attachment or deep, passionate intimacy, sex becomes boring and unsatisfying. This is where people get attracted to other individuals and affairs occur. The cheating spouse is looking for newness and excitement and falls into the false belief that the adrenaline is what being in love is all about. In response they go to their therapist with the phrase, 'I don't love him anymore.' But they don't understand that the newness passion is meant to wear off to instill a deeper intimacy with each other.

"Women are especially deceived in this way. They will come to me and say, 'Maybe I never did love him.' They start saying that over and over again, nurturing this thought and end up falling into adultery. They were never able to transfer their attraction to their husband to attachment with their husband.

"So the sex education class I took in preparation for marriage really helped Cliff and me during our first years together as we established sexual unity and passionate intimacy for each other. In turn, I was eventually able to move in a healthy way from attraction *to* Cliff to attachment *with* Cliff. It helped that we dated for four years and weren't sexual but developed our relationship as best friends and confidants.

"In today's society we try to do it backward. We start off having sex and then try to capture the friendship and intimacy, which complicates the relationship. It's muddied by all those feelings that come with the sex, making it more difficult for us to grow in deeper intimacy and care for each other.

"There are many couples out there, who, like Cliff and me, are learning how to please each other. Many women are having sex with their mate but are unable to receive pleasure. Sometimes that occurs out of lack of knowledge. The more that Cliff and I studied and prayed, the more we learned. When you learn how the body works, you can understand how to enjoy sex. One way to do this is for a woman to learn about her own body and in turn learn to respond to the feelings that are associated with it. When you become familiar with your body and are able to affirm and thank God for the feelings associated with the desires he gave you, you can enjoy intercourse.

"God created us to have sexual feelings, and we need to affirm them in our bodies. Most young women become familiar with themselves between the ages of eight and twelve in response to something external. An example would be if they ran across their dad's or brother's pornography. Because it is an external image that has stimulated the girl, her response to her sexuality is ingrained to be external. What can often occur in this situation is that the girl gets hooked on the external stimulation and needs that stimulus in order to get aroused or reach orgasm. The conflict that occurs later when she gets married is that in order to be orgasmic, she has to go back to that external stimuli to get satisfaction. For example, for many women it's seeing women's breasts that they saw in their dad's pornography. This is not the way God intended for us to get intimacy or sexual satisfaction.

"Other unhealthy sexual patterns for women are developed from sexual abuse. Recently I heard a woman share her testimony at church. She shared about incest from her father that had occurred to her when she was a child. As she shared, she said that when she was dating her husband she was really attracted to him and turned on until she got engaged. At that point she couldn't stop finding things wrong with the poor guy. She had some unhealthy patterns imprinted into her sexuality so many years earlier from her father. Until those issues have been addressed, she will continue to push her husband away.

"One of the unhealthy patterns imprinted on children who have been sexually abused is a heightened awareness of sex. They think they are different from everybody else. That belief breeds shame and confusion about knowing something that other kids don't know. And in some ways the child feels special, but in other ways, weird or uncomfortable. This child may grow up being promiscuous; or, on the other hand, they may sexually isolate themselves from the opposite sex. These women may not act on that intense drive and desire before marriage, but what often happens is that when they become engaged or get married, everything shuts down and all of that sexual intensity just goes away. No matter what they do, they can't seem to access it at all. It disappears because sex got connected with something wrong rather than something right, and now that it's right, they can't do it.

"With the victim of abuse or otherwise, the sexual relationship between a couple needs to be one of mutual respect and mutual responsibility as they decide what the boundaries are in their marriage bed. One of the instrumental things we learn throughout Scripture is one of mutuality between a husband and wife. There is always a giving of ourselves to each other with mutual respect. If your mate wants to engage in behavior that is uncomfortable to you, then you shouldn't do it. It might be an area where you want to grow and become comfortable, but you are not there yet.

"A negative example of this is couples watching pornography together. Cliff and I have been told repeatedly that pornography leads to better sex in a couple's marriage. And while secular research has shown that couples who watch pornography together do have much more exciting, erotic sexual experiences after watching pornography, they also reveal that over time they become less and less able to respond to each other. So it destroys the intimacy even though it creates a short-term elicit, erotic response. The external stimuli steals the internal intimacy.

"Many women are unable to have orgasms outside of manual or oral stimulation, and there is nothing wrong with that. But if you feel like you're less of a person or you want to learn how to have an orgasm, you can do that through a variety of different steps that Cliff and I have used that have proven successful. One is what we call the 'bridging technique,' where you take what is working and bridge it with what isn't working. For example, if the woman can stimulate herself clitorally during intercourse, that often can help her pair or bring together or bridge her sexual response with the intercourse experience.

"We have a clitoral, vaginal stimulation exercise that we give couples to do when they are together. First, set the timer for twenty minutes and do clitoral, vaginal stimulation. That's stimulating the vagina around the G-spot area and the clitoral area. When the timer goes off, stop. The reason for that is so that you aren't trying to have an orgasm but instead allow enough stimulation time for the intensity in the body to build. Learning to listen to your body will help.

"Some women, after years of telling themselves no to sexual intercourse have difficulty getting to yes after marriage. In this case you have to go through the process of giving yourself permission and accepting that sexual intimacy is a natural, fun part of yourself, an enjoyable part. This may include letting go of the thought that this is not ladylike. Sex with your mate is not about being ladylike. In fact, it's feminine to enjoy that intense erotic response in your body.

"It helps to know that an orgasm is a reflex response that gets triggered when there is enough buildup of sexual tension from effective stimulation and freedom to go after it without inhibition or fear of being out of control. We cannot will an orgasm, but we can encourage or resist it.

"Sexual arousal and release are conditioned responses. They are similar to falling asleep. For example, I had difficulty sleeping as an infant, so my parents would drive me in the car to get me to sleep. Even today I tend to fall asleep when riding in a car. Likewise, if as a child or young adolescent you learned to block intense sexual feelings as I did, you will as an adult unknowingly continue to stop your arousal before it leads to orgasm. Some women have learned to be orgasmic by rocking on their pillow like helping a child to fall asleep. As adults they often have no clue about how to transfer that form of stimulation into sex with their husband. Fortunately, if we have learned to respond or not respond in a certain way, we can retrain our bodies to respond differently.

"Many women, unable to have an orgasm, give up on the chance of ever having one. Initially, a woman may be excited and enjoy sex with her husband, but over time she will become numb, allowing less and less sexual intensity to build. Eventually she will agree to sex primarily for him. But God has designed our bodies to respond sexually *to each other,* and Scripture teaches and implies that men and women have sexual drives that need to be fulfilled in marriage. Having sex for the other person is not a picture of the mutuality taught in 1 Corinthians 7. Thus, being able to respond orgasmically is important for personal satisfaction, for marital fulfillment, and for biblical realization.

"If you have been trying to have an orgasm and nothing seems to work, you may need to obtain a medical evaluation and tune-up. If something is wrong physically, all the efforts in the world will never produce an orgasm. Start with a hormonal evaluation. You may need to request that your physician have your estrogen, progesterone, total testosterone, and free testosterone levels measured. If you are menopausal, hormone replacement therapy may prove beneficial. If you are on a birth control pill that is high in progestins, which suppress sexual desire and response, you should switch to a pill that is higher in estrogen and androgen (testosterone) activity.

"Other factors that may interfere with orgasm and require medical attention include childbirth trauma or pelvic surgery, low blood flow to the genitals due to smoking or cardiovascular problems, and medications for other conditions. For example, Prozac and other antidepressants are used to slow down a man's ejaculation and often make it difficult for a woman to have an orgasm. Work with your physician to find a medication that treats your depression but doesn't suppress sexual response. Other antidepressants work well in this situation.

The most successful tool that Cliff and I obtained was knowledge of God's Word and prayer. It makes a profound statement in your marriage when you pray together over intimacy and sexuality. Remembering that God created you both as sexual beings with the goal of intimacy will help you broach him with this topic. Doing so will assure Ecclesiastes 4:9–12 remains true: 'Two are better than one. . . . If one falls down, his friend can help him up. . . . If two lie down together, they will keep warm. But how can one keep warm alone? Though one may be overpowered, two can defend themselves. A cord of three strands is not quickly broken.'"

Eating Disorder

Featuring Nancy Alcorn

"For five years it was the worst bondage I've ever been in. It was five years of hell."

Nancy Alcorn

KAREN ANNE CARPENTER was one of the all-time great musical sensations of the 70s, capturing three Grammys, eight gold albums, ten gold singles, and five platinum albums. Gifted in both playing and singing, she held the record for the most top-five hits in the first year of business. On the stage she was glamorous and loved by the crowd. She guest-starred on TV shows, appeared on the front cover of many national magazines, and toured worldwide. Young girls looked up to her. She was a role model and a symbol of American culture. But amidst her fame and fortune, she was dying a self-destructive death known as anorexia nervosa.

On February 4, 1983, after years of starving herself and dieting, Karen was found unconscious on the floor of a walk-in closet in her mother's home. She was rushed to the hospital where attempts were made to save her life, but within an hour Karen died of cardiac arrest caused by the strain that the anorexia had put on her heart. Karen's widely publicized death was not the first one caused by the illness and would not be the last. Research reveals that seven to ten million American women and seventy million women worldwide are diagnosed annually with eating disorders. Without treatment, up to 20 percent of those women will die.

This is one woman's journey through that same disorder with a different ending. Nancy overcame anorexia nervosa, but it wasn't easy. Her struggle was cut short after she adamantly fought her own desire to self-destruct by submitting to God's will for her to live. This is her incredible story of how she overcame the disease that was eating at her soul.

"I was born and raised in a good churchgoing home in Tennessee, as the fourth child out of seven. Because there were so many children, my parents had to run a tight ship. In doing so, they expected a lot when I was growing up, and in turn, my brothers and sisters and I were taught to perform instead of just being ourselves. We pretended to be the perfect family and made sure we looked good on the outside. But inside the family there were a lot of unresolved issues, one of which was strife between family members.

"For example, when I was ten, my little sister, who was three and a half, was killed in a tractor accident on my family's farm. My dad had asked my mother to come out of the house and help him pull the tractor up out of the ditch. There was no one else to help him that day and no one to watch my sister. So my mom handed her to my dad, who sat her on his lap while my mom got in the truck to pull the tractor from the watery channel. As my mom pushed on the accelerator of the truck, both vehicles jackknifed, and the truck ended up on top of the tractor, crushing my sister between my dad and the steering wheel of the tractor. She was crushed to death right in his lap. It was a horrendous ordeal.

"Instead of talking about it and working through the grief after the funeral, we just pretended nothing had happened. There was so much trauma and unspoken pain in everyone's heart it was almost unbearable. I learned to suck it up and go on with life. I tried to be perfect, not to cause any problems. As a family, we got in a pattern of avoiding dealing with issues.

"I was in elementary school when the accident happened, and I remember being wracked with fear all the time. After something like that happens in your family, you panic every time you hear an ambulance or whenever somebody's late. Your mind runs with thoughts of the worst-case scenario. Fear was something I began to experience a lot of—fear over what we went through, fear of upsetting my parents, and fear about not doing well.

"Other dynamics in my family may have contributed to my eating disorder. With so many kids, there was already a feeling of being deprived. My parents made sure we always had plenty to eat. We weren't poor, but there were certain foods we just didn't get to eat very often, especially if they were expensive, like chicken. With so many people being at the table, we were always mindful that there were always eight other people eating, and there are only so many chicken legs, thighs, and breasts. My internal thought was, *You'd better grab it now because if you don't it's not going to be there later.*

"My parents always made taking us to church a priority, but I did not ask Jesus into my heart as a child. Anyone looking only at outward appearances would have believed I was a committed Christian. In high school I continued to attend church regularly with my family. If asked if I was a good Christian girl, any one of the adult members of my church would have replied, 'Oh, yes, of course she is. She's even president of the youth group.'

"Being president of my church's youth fellowship didn't mean a thing. I had not given my heart to Jesus. I was too busy living my life my own way. I did not understand who Jesus Christ was, what he had done for me, or what he would do for me if I would only ask him.

"As a result of going my own way, I felt increasingly empty and aimless. At first I didn't realize that my life lacked purpose. I was popular in school. I always had friends among the "in" crowd, and I was repeatedly elected to hold office in student government. From outward appearances there was nothing wrong with my life.

"Performance in athletic activities gave me value, and my self-esteem depended on my success in sports. From a relatively young age, sports was the center of my identity, and I planned my future around a career in athletics. I was continually involved in various athletic competitions at my school. I started for the ninth grade basketball team even though I was only in seventh grade. I already knew what I wanted to do with my life: play college basketball while majoring in physical education. I planned to become a coach or an athletic director. I took comfort in knowing where I was headed.

"But in ninth grade my world shattered. I seriously injured my knee, and every time it started to heal, I injured it again. I loved basketball so much I couldn't wait for my knee to heal properly before I got back on the court. I went to an orthopedic specialist at Saint Thomas Hospital in Nashville, who also happened to be the team physician for the Vanderbilt University Athletic Department. Since I was an avid Vanderbilt fan, I really thought that was a big deal and that he was the best. Dr. Lipscomb prescribed a weight-lifting regimen to rehabilitate my knee.

"I continued to injure my knee. Several times I ended up in Dr. Lipscomb's office after ill-fated attempts to play basketball. My knee would be tightly swollen and blue, and he would withdraw several syringes full of bloody fluid that had collected at the joint. Though I hated the pain I suffered and the horrible sight of what I was doing to my knee, I kept trying to play sports. My determination led to two major knee surgeries. Finally Dr. Lipscomb sat me down in his office and told me what I didn't want to hear, that I had to stop participating in sports all together.

"Sports was the one thing I knew I was good at, and basketball was my life. It was unimaginable to me that I could no longer play. As I realized I would never again be able to play basketball, I grew hopeless and bitter.

"Once I faced the fact that I could no longer play, in order to have something to do with the game I loved, I became the manager of the girls' basketball team. I went through intense emotional struggles before I could consent to carrying water bottles and distributing towels to the players. I hated being reduced to having such an unimportant and invisible position on the team. I was used to being at the center of attention on the court, not being stuck on the sidelines. It took everything in me to remain involved in the game as a supporter, and I was envious of the girls who were out on the court. Many times as I watched the team play, I wondered why I subjected myself to such agony. But I couldn't stand the thought of not being connected to the team in some way, so I stuck it out as water girl.

"Though I could still pursue a career in athletics as a coach or trainer, my immediate future seemed bleak because the possibility of playing college basketball had been snatched from me. I no longer had a driving goal to give my life meaning. Many of my girlfriends were hoping to find husbands and get married soon after high school. While I was not opposed to being a wife and mother, I did not want to marry young.

"In response to the anger I felt, I rebelled. I began to smoke and started drinking. I knew it was wrong, but at the time I didn't care. Since I would be unable to pursue my ambition of a life in sports, I no longer cared about staying in shape. As a result, I began to put on weight.

"I had always been weight conscious because I was playing sports and wanted to fit in. But after my injury I became inactive, causing my metabolism to slow down. Additionally, my body went through the normal teenage changes, and I wasn't completely prepared for that. The weight gain brought on feelings of insecurity about the way I looked in my clothes, and I grew even more self-conscious. I was already a bit insecure, and that just made it worse.

"As a result of my weight gain, I started depriving myself, trying to manipulate my body. For example, if I craved a hamburger, I'd eat a salad. The problem was that I'd eat three times more salad than normal because what I was really craving was a hamburger. In the end I would have been better off eating a hamburger. But I didn't think like that.

"One day I realized that despite cutting back on fatty foods, my clothes were getting too tight for me. I just felt like I didn't have control of what was going on around me and that I was getting heavier and heavier. I quickly fell into the mind-set that often exists among teenage girls: starving myself.

"I was so mad at myself for eating so much that I would punish myself, depriving myself of food completely. Eventually I'd break down and eat something, overeating again because I knew I'd starve myself afterward. It was a self-defeating, self-punishing behavior.

"Looking back, I can see that no one else really thought I was heavy. But for some reason, when I looked in the mirror, I saw a distorted, heavy person staring back at me. I didn't weigh more than 130 pounds at that time.

"About that time I had my first boyfriend. I was crazy about him. We went to a swimming pool with a bunch of our friends on a date and had a good time. Shortly after that he broke up with me. So I got his best friend to find out why. His response was devastating. He said my boyfriend didn't like the way I looked in a bathing suit.

"An uncle had said something similar to me once. He said, 'Getting a little pudgy there aren't you, Nancy?' He thought he was playing with me, but it crushed my already broken spirit. My ex-boyfriend's comment intensified that pain.

"I graduated high school at seventeen. I had long recognized the emptiness of the teenage drinking parties I occasionally attended. Not only were they unfulfilling; they were not exciting enough to overcome the oppressive lack of direction in my life. Furthermore, I knew what I was doing was not only wrong but against the standards I had set for myself throughout my teenage years. I had always been a leader, but by drinking and smoking, I was conforming to other people's standards and behaving more like a follower.

"While I was trying to cope with my aimlessness, other forces were working to give my life a direction different from anything I had imagined. I had a Christian friend who, though I was not aware of it at the time, had been praying for my conversion for three years. Cleta was a high school cheerleader who had been looking for an opportunity to witness to me.

"About three weeks before I was to leave for college, Cleta called me and invited me to a lay-witness meeting at church. I went, and for the first time in my life, I saw laypeople standing up in front of the church sharing their testimonies, bearing witness to what Jesus Christ had done in their lives.

"I was particularly moved by the messages of many of the young people who were there, explaining how they had been set free from sin, guilt, and fear and how Jesus Christ filled the void in their lives, giving them purpose and direction. The Holy Spirit began to convict me that I needed to repent, release my life to Christ, and rely on him in a day-to-day relationship.

"I left the church service that night struggling. I wasn't sure I wanted to make such a commitment. I was headed nowhere, and my life needed to be turned around, but I wasn't sure I was willing to give up my independence. I spent the next three days unable to either eat or sleep, under the strong conviction that I needed to ask God for a new life and for forgiveness of my sins. In the middle of the week, I decided to stop fighting against what I knew I needed to do.

"I gave my life to the Lord and spent the next three weeks until I went to college devouring the Bible. For the first time in my life, I could not put it down, reading it both day and night.

"I went to Middle Tennessee State University in Murfreesboro, Tennessee, and majored in physical education, but it seemed unfulfilling to me. I became interested in working with troubled girls and felt that I might want to be a counselor or possibly go into some type of criminal justice work.

"I continued to struggle with my eating disorder, becoming more and more obsessed about food. I would continually talk to my body, telling myself that I was going to starve it.

"I started college off by living in a dorm, and the other girls and I would pool our money and eat late-night pizza. I wanted to fit in, but I started to gain weight again. Additionally, weight was a common topic. We were always looking at magazines and comparing ourselves with one another. We would say, 'Let me see if I can get in your jeans,' or 'Can you get in this dress?' and, 'Don't you wish you looked like this girl in this magazine?' or, 'Like that girl that lives across the hall?' Comparing myself to others brought intense anxiety and pressure to fit in.

"I noticed that I had a tendency to overeat any time that I felt anxious or stressed. It could be a test in one of my classes, or even when I had done something I wasn't proud of. The fear of getting fat was so intense that I eventually moved out with a few girls, and we got our own apartment.

"The talk about our bodies and the comparison continued. We'd go on low-carb diets and do crazy stuff to lose weight fast. I did lose weight, but the second I stopped the diet, I'd gain it all back. Being on the no-carb diet fed my eating disorder because I could eat as much steak, cheese, and eggs that I wanted. Eventually though, I'd get sick of the same food and would binge on something I was really craving, starting the cycle of bingeing and deprivation all over again.

"The lack of grain and fiber in my diet caused me to develop a problem with constipation, among other things. Then both my weight and emotions went up and down, up and down, up and down. I became addicted to the low-carb diet. I would reach a point where I'd say, 'I don't want to deprive myself of food anymore. I can't stand the deprived feeling, so if I want to lose weight, I'll just go on this Atkins diet because I can eat as much cheese and eggs and meat as I want.' The feeling of deprivation was a strong fear.

"Several of my roommates had eating disorders also. Like the dynamics in my own home growing up, none of us addressed it with the others. Sometimes someone would say, 'Why were you in the bathroom for so long?' But a simple answer about constipation would end the conversation. I made sure that I turned the water on in the sink and shower so I could cover up my secret. I wanted everybody to think that I was the perfect girl, with no problems, and a perfect Christian. So I hid it because it was all a perfectionism thing. Trying to have the perfect body, trying to be the perfect Christian, trying to be the perfect person with the most perfect behavior.

"After graduating from college, I did an internship at a women's prison. I continued the cycle of dieting and deprivation. I was working for the state, and I started doing street ministry and volunteering with Teen Challenge. One evening I went to my pastor's house for dinner. They were going to a meeting, and, in an attempt to get their approval, I offered to stay and clean up the kitchen.

"They willingly accepted the offer and went on to their meeting. I had eaten too much and was feeling nauseous, but I knew I only had so much time to get the house clean. So I decided to make myself throw up so I'd feel better and be able to finish cleaning the kitchen. Thus began a five-year struggle with bulimia.

"I bought into the lie that I could continue to indulge in the cycle of gorging and purging. The day I started at my pastor's house, I remember hearing a voice say, 'You can do this all the time, and you can eat anything you want.'

"Eventually I came across a book that defined my eating disorder as bulimia, but until then no one really talked about it. Lack of education about the illness encouraged the behavior because I didn't know what I was doing to my body. Additionally, I was serving the

Lord, so it was easy to justify that overall I was a good girl, minimizing my eating disorder. I was a Christian peer in my singles group, and I didn't want to share it with anyone. It was that cycle of silence that I learned as a kid. I wanted everyone to see me as the good Christian girl.

"But after five years of struggling with bulimia, my body was in chaos. My face was swollen, my eyes were puffy and bloodshot, and I had constant constipation and severely irregular periods. I was depressed and getting to a place where no matter how much I tried I still gained weight.

"I knew I had to find a way to escape the hell I'd put myself in. The only way out, I reasoned, was by diligently crying out to God and washing myself in the Word. I knew I was living a dual life, pretending to be someone I wasn't, and I couldn't do it anymore. I started to cry out to God with a new desperation. I'd say, 'God, please show me how to get out of this. Teach me how to eat because it scares me to think about eating. Don't you understand? It's Monday, and I'm scared about eating at a cookout on Saturday!'

"This meant that I had to let go of control and allow God to be in control. It was a hard place to be after living a life with a façade. Behind the mask of perfection, I found extreme fear—fear of being insecure, fear about not being able to please people, fear that I would lose control, fear of gaining weight, and rigid rules and regulations to keep me living there.

"About that time God gave me a picture in my mind that I will never forget. It was an image of a fireplace. The fire inside was raging so fast that if you put another log on it, the fire would consume the log instantly. Then he showed me another fireplace where there was a smoldering fire with just a flicker of color as it burned slowly.

Then he spoke to my heart and said, 'This is what your metabolism is doing now.' Instead of burning up the fuel, it has slowed down to a point that it can't burn anything. Normal metabolism burns like the first fire.'

"So I asked him what I should do. He taught me to listen to what my body was saying opposed to telling it what to do. If I was craving a hamburger, eat it but work toward regulating my intake and the timing of my food consumption. Basically, he taught me to eat when I was hungry without gorging. I threw out my scales and began to exercise in moderation as God led.

"God was faithful to my cries and walked with me through the healing of my fears. I became faithful because he was first faithful to me. I learned a new freedom from God that I'd never experienced previously. And what's amazing is that I lost weight, dropping to a natural size for my body type within a year's time.

"As I worked toward healing, I distinctively remember hearing God say to me, 'If you will do this my way and let me free you, I will make you the size that you are supposed to be. I created you; I know what's best. But if you keep trying to do it by your own efforts, you are going to keep falling on your face, and you will be miserable.'

"So every time I walked, exercising, I visualized the fire being full, burning the logs continually. Through that I learned that God could be trusted. There is one verse that spoke the loudest to me in that time. It was 2 Timothy 1:7. It says, 'For God did not give us a spirit of timidity, but a spirit of power, of love, and of self-discipline.'"

Leaving Lesbianism Behind

Featuring Anne Paulk

"I liked having the attention she gave me when I was in the role of a boy. It was the beginning of a lifelong identity struggle that would eventually become a fierce game of tug-of-war inside of me."

Anne Paulk

STUDIES REVEAL THAT 4 percent of the population struggles with exclusive homosexuality. That number increases dramatically when bisexuality is considered. Lesbianism has been a predominantly hidden secret in the body of Christ, with victims of homosexuality fearing rejection and hatred. Additionally, fear has kept the church from reaching out in ministry to those caught in this web of deceit.

Anne Paulk, the woman featured in this story, has done research and found that in her own study, 97 percent of gay respondents said they attended church. When asked how frequently, over one-half answered weekly, with the remainder reporting attendance several times a week. Thus, it is obvious that homosexuality is not a secret that can remain so. Instead, the festering that causes the wound of lesbianism needs to be broken and healed. This is Anne's inspiring story about how she obtained healing and how others can do the same.

"I was born in 1963 in Lewiston, Idaho, during the women's liberation movement. From early childhood until I was about four years old, I had a normal, healthy childhood. Like most little girls, I played with dolls, tried to look pretty, and looked and acted like a feminine little girl. My mother dressed me in cute dresses and enrolled me in ballet and tap lessons. One of my favorite things to do was to play with my Barbie doll.

"I lived in a stable home where my father worked and my mother was a housewife, and I was blessed to get the benefit of having a nurturing mother around from birth. She had grown up in the Great Depression, never finished high school, and had poor identity about herself as a woman. Despite her own childhood, she was a caring and loving mother.

"My father was a hard-working, loving man who taught me early on that I was special. We were close, and he often lovingly called me 'Daddy's girl.' But for some reason unknown to me, instead of continuing in that pattern, he stopped. I didn't know why, so I internalized it as rejection and began to look for ways to regain his attention. Parents have a tremendous influence on the formation of a child's self-perception. And, for me, my father's silence spoke volumes.

"Shortly after this shift, during the summer months when school was out, something else occurred that would intensify the already existing feelings of rejection and insignificance I was experiencing. My sister and I were bored and decided to explore our own neighborhood for something to do. We ended up at a neighbor's house, playing with a friend. She had a fourteen-year-old brother, and while bouncing a tennis ball against the wall, it had rolled into his room and under his bed. I willingly ran into the room in search of the ball, rummaging under his bed.

"As I was searching, I noticed something sticking out from under the mattress. Curious, I pulled it out and stared at it for a moment. It was a pornographic magazine featuring page after page of nude women who were exposing themselves in shocking ways. I noticed that there were several magazines hidden under the mattress, and I managed to look at two or three before my sister started calling my name. In fear, I stuffed the magazines back where I found them and left the room.

"Over the next few days I thought about the pictures I'd seen. They intrigued me, and I continually replayed the slide show of photographs in my four-year-old mind. I told my friend about her brother's magazines, which stimulated her curiosity, so we began looking at them together. One day I approached her brother and asked about the magazines. He took it as an opportunity and offered to 'show me something more.'

"The boy and I played a hide-and-seek game with a flashlight that always ended with me touching his genitals. I didn't understand that he was being sexually aroused and certainly had no idea he was using me for his own ends. What I did know was that after I became bored with the game and left, I felt dirty and ashamed. I didn't understand what had happened, but in the depth of my heart, I knew that I had participated in something very wrong. As a result, I felt vulnerable, unprotected, and exposed. I yearned to talk about my feelings to someone, but the boy had warned me that we would both be in trouble if I did. So I remained silent about what had taken place.

"My silence turned inward, and I started having recurring dreams and nightmares about the abuse. As minor as the experience seemed, it had traumatized my fragile soul, and because I'd internalized it, my mind was processing it through my sleep. To the core of my being, I felt powerless and defenseless, and the nightmares haunted my sleep. I sensed there was nothing I could do to prevent other sexual trespasses from happening again. I closed myself off emotionally and subconsciously put up barriers against ever feeling so unsafe again.

"Meanwhile, another unexpected event shook my world; my beloved grandpa died. I had been very close to my grandfather. My sister and I loved him so much that we often vied for the position of sitting closest to him. I had felt safe and protected by him for as long as I could remember and knew beyond a doubt that he really loved and adored me as his special little girl. He was a man who had reinforced my femininity by loving me so freely and without expectations. When he died, I was at a loss.

"My grandfather's death was devastating to my mother as well. He was her rock. After his death, I began to notice that my mother would say negative things about herself, like saying she was stupid. I started to feel and act like I was the mother and she was the child. I'd assure her that she wasn't stupid but smart. I'd comfort her and be her confidante in times of difficulty. From my perspective, she seemed like a piece of debris floating wherever the tide took her. As I watched this, I thought, *I don't want to be like you. You don't have it going on. You're not exciting.* My perception of womanhood was distorted, believing all women were like her—weak, fragile, and insecure. As I matured, I learned to value education and even grew to dislike my mother because she was uneducated.

"Events followed that deteriorated the seed of femininity inside of me. One example was in elementary school when a boy I was friends with complained about having a headache. Like I'd seen my mother do when my father had a headache, I began to rub the boy's shoulders. It was an innocent gesture of compassion. The reaction of my teachers was harsh, that I had done something inappropriate. They yelled at me, scolded, and punished me profusely. Then my teachers called my parents and told them what had happened. I felt deeply ashamed, internalizing the false belief that liking boys was dangerous and humiliating.

"To further complicate things, I was inept at social skills. I was quiet, terminally shy, and deathly afraid of failure. Those qualities helped lock me in my prison of silence and insecurity. As the weeks and months went by, I became increasingly masculine looking. I totally rejected the female identity and didn't look anything like the little girl I'd once been. I was moving closer and closer to looking like a boy. I was so insecure about my identity that I hated recess and lunch, longing to go back to class, even though I didn't enjoy schoolwork either.

"Shortly after I began to move toward a more masculine identity, I met another third-grader named Carolyn. We had so much fun together that we even spent time after school playing. Our families soon got to know one another, which gave us a lot of time to be together. One day Carolyn suggested that we pretend that we were each other's boyfriends. We were hooked on teen magazines and both had a crush on Donny Osmond. So when she suggested that I be Donny and she'd be the girlfriend, I accepted the offer. I enjoyed pretending I was a boy. It gave me the initiative to be in control of a situation and gave me a false confidence.

"Carolyn and I began to kiss each other as we played this game repeatedly. I liked having the attention she gave me when I was in the role of a boy. It was the beginning of a lifelong identity struggle that would eventually become a fierce game of tug-of-war inside of me.

"I continued to look at pornography and was soon in a full-fledged addiction. I found out that my brother had a stash of magazines in his room, and I'd eagerly await opportunities to view the pages of naked women. I would read the strange stories and peer at the sexually explicit photographs. I was fascinated by their bodies and eventually began to feel aroused by looking at the women.

"The summer of 1972, our family left Idaho, moving to Pennsylvania. There my parents began taking us to a Presbyterian church. I didn't mind starting over in a new state except for one little problem: I was desperately homesick for Carolyn.

"About a year later I met a girl named Laura who lived down the street from me. I was about ten, and she was a year younger. While she seemed secure and content about being a little girl, I continued to look and act boyish. Eventually the two of us got into the kissing game I had played with Carolyn. Unlike the experience with Carolyn, Laurie and I fell into a sensual experience. In fact, she began to touch me sexually in my genitals. One day Laurie's mother came in and caught us in the act, and that was the end of our game. Laurie's mother demanded that I go home, and she indignantly reported to my mother what had taken place. When my mother questioned me, I told her I had felt strange about the whole thing and that Laurie had come up with the idea.

"Later that year my friend Carolyn moved to New York. It was a substantial drive away, but because our families were friends, we got together now and then. Carolyn and I quickly resumed our kissing game. By now we were both becoming more mature, and her interest was more toward boys. But in our imaginary game, her allure was acted out toward me. As a result, I was attracted to her as a lesbian, but she was attracted to me by pretending I was a boy. It was a sad form of intimacy, and although it was unsatisfying for me, it was intensely addictive.

"The following summer my family went on a vacation along the East Coast. As we visited various points of interest, I became aware that people couldn't tell I was a girl. My grooming, posture, clothing, and hairstyle all gave them the impression from a distance that I was a boy. I found this humiliating.

"One day as I walked out of a gas station restroom, a woman, waiting her turn, accused me of being in the wrong bathroom. Tears burned my eyes, and I flushed red with shame. It had never been my conscious intention to look like a boy. My masculine style was just a cover-up for my feelings—a thick, impenetrable barrier to protect myself. And the older I got, the more pronounced my gender confusion became. My physical appearance became more of a hindrance than protection.

"Relationships with other girls continued to occur. It began with me noticing, then fantasizing about them. Such was the case with Julie. From the first day we met in my junior-high French class, I was attracted to her. To my delight she and I became friends and began to spend a lot of time together.

"As we got to know each other, I became convinced that Julie would be a wonderful life partner. I started to imagine what it would be like to be married to her. One day I told her that I loved her so much that I wanted to marry her. Instantly Julie withdrew from our relationship, and I was no longer welcome to spend time with her or go to her home.

"I graduated from high school and began college right away. I continued to reject my identity as a girl, wearing clothes that hid my figure and reinforced my attempt at attaining a masculine identity. One day as I was jogging through campus, some guys at a frat house whistled. While I'm sure they meant it as a compliment, I was terrified, feeling an intense need to hide myself. From that point on I made an effort to run more like a man by sticking out my elbows and wearing baggy clothes to conceal my figure. Looking back, I can see that I feared being devoured by a man, feeling extremely unsafe as a woman.

"At college I found different women to be involved with intimately as I matured and physically grew into womanhood. The result was always the same. I'd become obsessed with someone, they'd eventually drop me, and I'd be sick at heart, unable to deal with the loss. The loneliness and pain of being alone tortured me relentlessly. In an effort to find healing from my repeatedly broken heart, I sought counseling from a gay peer counselor.

"My therapist was a gay Catholic. Although I had little understanding of the Christian faith, I'd heard enough to know that most Christians believe homosexuality is wrong, and the idea of being on the wrong side of God nagged at me.

"'Look,' I explained to my counselor, 'I'm really having trouble with my lesbian feelings. I've read passages in the Bible about Sodom and Gomorrah, and I just don't know what to do.'

"The man smiled kindly at me, nodding his head in understanding, and said, 'The important thing for you to understand is that you can be a Christian and still be gay. The Bible isn't really against homosexuality. God is love, and the Bible never speaks against love of any kind. The story you read is in the Old Testament. Jesus said to love your neighbor, and that's what homosexual attractions really are—love.'

"As much as I wanted to believe him, I couldn't accept his interpretation of the Scripture passages. On the other hand, I felt no obligation to obey the Bible. To me, God seemed like a vague, distant concept, nothing but an illusion blocking my way to happiness with a lifetime woman lover. I decided to whisk everything under a rug and simply proclaim that God didn't exist. I concluded that I had to throw him completely away in order to pursue what I wanted. I knew that I'd never find fulfillment in lesbianism if I tried to fit it into a world where God was in charge.

"Before long I began to have dreams about Jesus. I began to take these dreams to heart, asking my friends who Jesus was and who he said he was. One day I ran into a woman named Lynn. She was outgoing, and I would often find her talking with the utmost gentleness, kindness, and respect to those not welcome in the "in" crowd. Her kindness was attractive to me, and I began to fantasize about her, wondering if she too were a lesbian. But when I asked a friend of hers about her, I learned that she was a Christian. Her faith, however, didn't deter my feelings for her. One day after class, I introduced myself to her.

"We struck up a friendship and began to spend time together. Lynn seemed to like having me around. We went for walks on the beach and spent time together that I saw as romantic. I told her I was a lesbian, and she admitted that she'd had lesbian desires before. She responded a little to my advances. As a result, my feelings became overpowering. One day I told her I loved her and wanted to marry her.

"She smiled and looked deeply into my eyes. I saw deep compassion and tenderness as she said, 'You know, Anne, I'm really married to Jesus. I do care for you as a friend, but my heart has to be committed to Christ.' Her response set a clear boundary for me. In the midst of my disappointment, I also felt a little relieved that I wasn't losing our friendship.

"We continued our friendship and spent a great deal of time together. But I found myself confused with her ambivalence. She said she loved and was married to Christ, but she allowed me to embrace her. We would also study lying on the bed together. She brought me roses on occasion and wrote affectionate notes, seeming to play a romantic game of cat and mouse, a game I was eager to play.

"I continued to have dreams about Jesus and eventually signed up for a class in evangelism training. I was curious about Lynn's relationship with God and had questions about his identity. I learned that there's a spiritual realm and an evil being named Satan who is bent on wreaking havoc. I asked every question I could think of, and someone always had a sensible answer.

"I was asked by the Campus Ambassadors leader to pray one day. I made an effort to sound like all the other students. I wanted so much to fit in with the group. One night as we bowed our heads, I felt a presence that seemed to permeate the room. An incredible being, the Holy Spirit, had enveloped us in gentleness, kindness, authority, reliability, and credibility. But I also sensed that I was on the outside looking in. I thought, *They have what I want. I know that's what I want. I don't care about anything else in my life. I want that more than anything, including homosexuality.*

"After the meeting I talked to the pastor, explaining to him what I felt. He asked what was holding me back, so I explained to him that I was gay but wanted the presence of God. He nodded his head thoughtfully and replied, 'Well, that's a bit of a conflict, Anne. There's nothing to prevent you from accepting God's grace. It's just that you can't continue to have it both ways. You are either going to surrender your life to Christ or you're not.'

"I told him I understood, and he told me how to ask Jesus into my heart but warned me that Satan wouldn't give up on me easily. He wrote his phone number on a piece of paper and said that I could call him day or night and he'd pray with me.

"I went home feeling nervous because I knew I had to do it. I knelt down by my bed and prayed, asking Jesus into my heart as my Savior. Temptation followed as I shared with my lesbian friends about the decision I'd made. But ironically, the biggest temptation came from my friend Lynn. Although she still maintained that she was married to Christ, her feelings for me seemed to change. Now, as a believer, I had something more to offer. With Christ's new life within me, I became more attractive to her, and she was becoming sexually interested in me.

"After learning about my decision to follow Jesus, some women associated with Campus Ambassadors taught me more about the Bible and prayer. I was open with them about my struggle with lesbianism. Their response of love and acceptance, tinted with the truth in God's Word, led me to continue to grow in Christ. My pastor referred me to a good counselor who was a believer and was experienced with working with people who were gay. I was able to see how the events in my life helped shape my distorted view of myself and began to heal from the sexual abuse I'd incurred as a child.

"My senior year of college, I transferred to Cal State Hayward to finish my education. At the beginning of that year, I met a young master's student named Mary. She was a bright, attractive woman who was a devout Christian. Mary was amazing, and from the instant I met her, I wanted her to be my best friend.

"Like me, Mary was searching for intimacy and a deep connection with another person. She had no lesbianism in her background, but she knew that I had been a lesbian and continued to have lesbian feelings.

"Mary lived off campus in an old farmhouse where Campus Ambassadors often held twenty-four-hour prayer meetings. Many nights Mary and I would talk into the wee hours of the morning. Eventually, when we did go to bed, Mary allowed me to sleep in the same single bed, cuddled up with her. In our minds we justified that because there was no sexual contact, we weren't sinning.

"From time to time we wrote each other notes, gave each other flowers, and acted romantic toward each other. I knew that I was growing more and more attracted to her. One day I told her that if we ever engaged in sexual activities, I was going to leave her because I feared losing my relationship with God.

"Meanwhile, my friend Lynn reentered my life. She wanted to take me out for dinner and celebrate my birthday. The evening of celebration came, and she showed up with a beautiful card. She had arranged for flowers—a dozen yellow roses—to be waiting for me at a romantic restaurant.

"Despite my closeness with Mary, I still dreamed about Lynn. She had always been my fantasy, but she also refused to take things to the next level because of her marriage to Christ. But that night was different; there was no mistaking the change. Lynn looked beautiful. She was attentive and affectionate and was clearly romancing me.

"After dinner we drove up to the beach to look at the stars. I had recently become a Christian and had committed myself to following Jesus regardless of my feelings, but I was being presented with an opportunity I'd dreamed about for years. And, I reasoned, had been in my life first, even before Jesus. My dream of having sex with Lynn and having her as my life partner seemed to be becoming a reality.

"I shared with her my desire to kiss her, and she encouraged me to do so. It was the first time she had ever been open to an advance from me. Rather than pushing me away, she embraced me, and we began to caress each other. We didn't get far, though. Unexpectedly and suddenly, I had the most overwhelming sensation that Jesus was there and could see perfectly well what was going on. How could I betray him after all he had done for me?

"I pulled away and told Lynn that I couldn't follow through in the direction we were headed. I wanted something else. Later I tried to talk to Lynn about her relationship with the Lord. I had learned that she was getting involved with other women, and I was concerned about her. She continued to pursue homosexuality and has been in that lifestyle since.

"Mary was supportive of my decision and came alongside me, exuding strength when I was feeling weak and broken. She comforted me emotionally and encouraged me spiritually, but our relationship teetered on inappropriate intimacy. I was so unhealthy that I couldn't see how unnatural and misguided it was.

"Mary eventually got her master's degree, and we moved away from each other. Absent from her, I longed to recapture the wonderful Christian nurturing I'd lost while pursuing our relationship. Fortunately, about that time, InterVarsity college ministry brought a woman to the Hayward campus to start a Christian fellowship.

"I immediately revealed my struggle to her and told her about the kind of support I thought I needed. Together we started organizing a group to help others like me. At our first meeting, I met a girl named Melissa who had a butch haircut but was more feminine than I was. Little by little the two of us developed a friendship.

"Mary's absence had opened a huge hole in my life, and Melissa instinctively tried to fill it. Melissa also had a real relationship with Christ, but she lacked close friendships. Because she was so affectionate and so devoted to me, she gradually began to fill the void that Mary had left.

"Even though we enjoyed some enduring times together, Melissa was becoming increasingly jealous. I watched as she competed for my attention. She did everything she could to gain my favor. And it should have been easy; the one she was competing with was thousands of miles away.

"Summer arrived, and with it came my college graduation. Mary had moved to China and asked me to visit her for six weeks. I went with the expectation of rekindling our relationship. However, it didn't take me more than a couple of days with Mary to discover that she had developed a close relationship with a Chinese national, a woman named Han. After a few days of relentless disappointment, feeling battered and broken, I left Mary early.

"The more I thought about it, the more I blamed God. As far as I was concerned, he had yanked the rug out from under my feet emotionally. How could he have allowed Mary and me to become so close and then let her establish the same kind of relationship with another woman? My whole world was turned upside down. Because I'd never seen my relationship with Mary for what it really was, I couldn't comprehend God's purposes in allowing it to end. Instead,

I raged against him, lost in grief over what felt like a double betrayal: both Mary and God had forsaken me.

"After that trip to China, I remained bitter toward God. I stopped talking to him for a year. That estrangement left me open to act however I wanted, without consulting or obeying him.

"Because of my rebellion, Melissa and I began to have intense sexual tension between us. One night as we were staying in the same room at a friend's house, she kissed me on the lips, then pulled me on top of her. In the moments that followed, we initiated our long-awaited sexual relationship. What was amazing is that I felt no conviction.

"All my childhood dreams had suddenly come true, yet it was even better than that. In my relationship with Melissa, I was a woman, and didn't even have to pretend to be a man. The sex was great as far as feelings of stimulations and fulfillment were concerned. But we were playing a game, hiding the truth from other people—a secret that would eventually take its toll.

"Guilt began to plague me to the point that I frequently told Melissa that we needed to call off our relationship. Afraid of losing me, she'd threaten to commit suicide. Manipulated by her threats, I stayed in the relationship.

"Instead of breaking up, Melissa and I began a process of resisting, then giving in, then resisting again. But our resistance wasn't strong. Our feelings and our physical desires took charge every time. My flesh wanted satisfaction; my heart wanted Melissa. It was a heavy, hopeless battle.

"At last I came to see that I hadn't dealt with any of the issues that drew me toward women. There were any number of aspects of my gender confusion about which I needed to ask and accept other people's help. My troubles weren't going to be solved through Bible study and prayer alone. My problem was deeper than I thought. It was unmanageable. Lesbianism was no longer a pattern of thought or behavior that I could control.

"During those months I became aware of one wonderful truth: God doesn't desert a person who is in habitual sin. He continued to deal with me on a deep level, even in the midst of my sin. At the end of four months of sexual activity with Melissa, I turned to God and said, 'God, I love this sin. I *love* this sin. It feels so fulfilling. There's no way, if it's offered to me, that I can turn it down now because it's the fulfillment of all my dreams. It's an addiction, and I can't say no. You are going to have to do something. I want you to be the first love of my life, and I know you aren't right now. You're going to have to change my heart and make the changes for me.'

"And that's just what he did. A couple of days later, because of my guilt, I confessed everything to my InterVarsity leader, mistakenly believing she already knew about Melissa and me. The poor woman was clueless. When Melissa came in after the phone call, I told her I'd shared the truth. She was livid.

"Melissa and I soon met with some InterVarsity leaders who told us we needed to give up our relationship immediately. The anger with God that I'd felt about losing Mary was stirred up again. Now it seemed I was losing Melissa too. After that meeting I got into my car and wept inconsolably. I prayed, 'God, it's happening again. She's the only one who really knows me. And once again I'm losing the person who really understands me, the love I was looking for!'

"That was the end of my relationship with Melissa and the beginning of my healing. I didn't know it then, but I was about to become a new person. But the change didn't come easily, and for me it certainly didn't happen overnight.

"I began attending Exodus meetings, a Christian twelve-step group for homosexuals who are striving to leave the lifestyle behind. In addition, I began attending a Bible study group at church where I could be really honest about my struggles. I felt a great deal of support from those around me. Their encouragement upheld my desire to follow Jesus out of all the confusion between my sexual and my spiritual desires. For the first time I recognized that I really need the help and prayers of others.

"For months I had to bring every thought to Christ. My feelings for the lesbian lifestyle where consuming and addictive, and it was a hard area to move away from. Over time, though, that process made me mentally disciplined enough to displace all lesbian thoughts.

"In April 1988, I visited the women at the Love in Action live-in program and spent the weekend to see if I was interested in moving through a continued healing. I decided to join the live-in program the next year. Shortly after my decision I went to a Michael Card concert. There, as Michael prayed, in my mind I heard God speaking to me. He said, 'I will heal you, Anne. I want to heal you.' I walked out of there no longer wondering if someone can really leave homosexuality. I now had the assurance that God was doing it in me.

"I entered the program as planned and began working seriously on my issues. The more I examined the various factors and feelings involved in my infatuation, the less I was attracted to other women. My leaders helped me work through some tough issues, specifically why I was attracted to other women.

"One thing I learned about change is that it's a process. It takes work, time, and utter dependence upon God. I had a lot to learn.

For example, I had to learn the basics of communication with other women that wasn't centered around trying to find out their sexual orientation. When I initially met someone, I'd ask myself, 'Is this person attracted to me?' There was a deep, underlying deception within me that believed I would feel better about myself if I could have sex with another woman. I believed if another woman found me to be a wonderful person, then I was a wonderful person. I grappled with wanting others to tell me who I was. Even after I was committed to change, I had to rewire my thought patterns.

"One of the most instrumental things I grasped was that there was a distinct pattern of attraction I had for a specific type of lesbian woman. The common attraction was everything I wasn't but wanted to be.

"I learned that really good friendships are built over time, slowly and non-obsessively, and that healthy relationships grow through misunderstandings, disappointment, and forgiveness.

"Additionally, I found out that it is not unusual for women who have been abused or experienced painful childhood abuse to turn to other women opposed to the opposite sex. In fact, one of the common issues of lesbian women is that there has been an external and then internal devaluing of key females and femininity during childhood demonstrated by a definite rejection of their mother as a role model, a greater desire to emulate male role models, and the fact that before the age of thirteen most have felt somewhere between ambivalent to greatly disliking even being a girl.

"Gender role rejection is a deliberate, almost constant, and somewhat inflexible adoption of male interests and attributes by a female child, and something I could clearly relate to.

"What's amazing to me, as I have gone on to walk in freedom and even help others walk through freedom, is that despite the painful events of their lives, most women are strongly motivated to change by personal religious beliefs. It took me approximately two years to work through this change.

"One of my difficulties in coming out of the lesbian lifestyle was that Christians didn't know what to do with me. I just didn't fit into the normal mold. But I believe that if the church will take heed to this, there can be even more healing. Because of the lack of support, I had to seek other ministries to help me.

"When God mends a broken life, he often uses the experiences of those who have walked a similar path. As the apostle Paul writes, 'Praise be to the God and Father of our Lord Jesus Christ, the Father of compassion and the God of all comfort, who comforts us in all our troubles, so that we can comfort those in any trouble with the comfort we ourselves have received from God' (2 Cor. 1:3–4).

"When we've experienced the goodness of God, we want others to know his love too. For that reason, I would be amiss if I didn't take the opportunity to discuss the primary source of healing available to lesbian women—coming to know Christ personally.

"If you're a woman dealing with same-sex attraction, there is good news. God's goal for you is good. You may be accustomed to being hurt, to having relationships go wrong, to struggling with the pain of your past. Sometimes it's hard to believe that life can get better. But other women, myself included, have found a life that is infinitely better than anything we've experienced before as we've responded to Christ's invitation to a new life. We've turned from chasing the illusion of lesbianism to the reality of the only One who can comfort us completely, the Lord Jesus Christ.

"Perhaps you have been a lesbian long enough to have discovered that same-sex relationships eventually leave you empty and feeling tremendous loss. Meanwhile, the craving for true intimacy continues to recur. We all share a deep thirst for a satisfying relationship that lasts.

"The good news is that through Christ, God has made a way for us to be given a new life. All we have to do is put up the white flag, surrender ourselves to him, and accept God's provision for our deepest needs—Jesus. From then on, life becomes a process of learning to live through the power of Jesus Christ in us.

"If the lesbian lifestyle has left you tired and weighed down, you will delight in the invitation of Christ: 'Come to me, all you who are weary and burdened, and I will give you rest. Take my yoke upon you and learn from me, for I am gentle and humble in heart, and you will find rest for your souls. For my yoke is easy and my burden is light' (Matt. 11:28–30).

"Through the power and kindness of God, countless lesbian women have found security and delight in their identity as females despite horrendous childhoods and damaging choices in adulthood. These women also have discovered that God is the Great Restorer. He more than makes up for all we've missed while pursuing our lesbian lifestyle. And as if that isn't enough, he then allows us the joy of offering comfort to others who are troubled by the choices they have made.

"God gives a new life to those who seek him. Trust in him and his promise in Joel 2:25–26: 'I will repay you for the years the locusts have eaten. . . . You will have plenty to eat, until you are full, and you will praise the name of the LORD your God, who has worked wonders for you; never again will my people be shamed.'"

Notes

Chapter 2, Living with Regrets

1. David Frum, *The Right Man: The Surprise Presidency of George W. Bush* (New York: Random House, 2003), 283.

Chapter 7, Overcoming Sexual Abuse

1. Department of Health and Human Services, Administration for Children and Families, Child Maltreatment, 1995.

Chapter 8, Combating Pornography

1. Zogby Survey, Focus on the Family, 2002.